BRITAIN IN OLD PHOTOGRAPHS

LEIGHTON BUZZARD & LINSLADE

WITH HEATH & REACH, EGGINGTON, STANBRIDGE & BILLINGTON

MAUREEN BROWN & JUNE MASTERS

SUTTON PUBLISHING LIMITED

Sutton Publishing Limited
Phoenix Mill · Thrupp · Stroud
Gloucestershire · GL5 2BU

First published 1998

British Library Cataloguing in Publication Data
A catalogue record for this book is available from the
British Library.

ISBN 0-7509-0871-8

Typeset in 10/12 Perpetua.
Typesetting and origination by
Sutton Publishing Limited.
Printed in Great Britain by
Ebenezer Baylis, Worcester.

CONTENTS

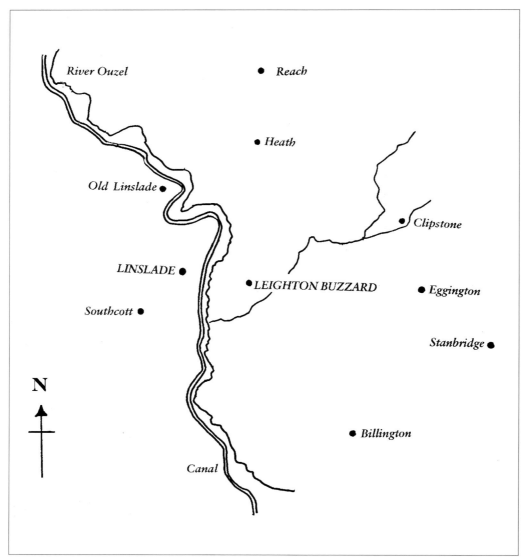

Map of the Leighton Buzzard and Linslade area.

INTRODUCTION

Leighton-Linslade today is a busy modern town, with the green ribbon of the Ouzel river valley and the Grand Union Canal running through its centre. The crossing over the river, which today is only important as a bottle-neck, was the reason for the siting of both Leighton Buzzard and Linslade, which until 1965 were two separate centres. The 'Buzzard' comes from Theobald de Busar, prebendary of Leighton in the late twelfth century. The Sussex 'Buzzard' was added to distinguish it from Leighton Bromswold, another church in the diocese of Lincoln.

In earliest times rivers provided the most basic necessity of life, water. They were also both a means of transport and a barrier, often forming boundaries between estates, and the Ouzel became the county boundary between Bedfordshire and Buckinghamshire. Crossing places attracted travellers, and subsequently developed into markets. Leighton Buzzard was settled by the seventh century and became a Royal estate. Linslade is described in a tenth-century charter and was also a Royal estate. At the Domesday survey in 1086 Leighton was the richest market in Bedfordshire, worth more than either Luton or Bedford. Included within its Domesday entry, though not named, were its hamlets of Heath and Reach, Eggington, Stanbridge and Billington.

Heath and Reach to the north of Leighton was probably once two separate hamlets strung out along the road connecting Leighton to Watling Street. Roman pottery was discovered at the Double Arches sandpit to the west of the village during the 1930s. The two names first appear in the thirteenth century, and the manor house at Heath, with its chapel nearby, probably dates from the fifteenth century.

Eggington and Clipstone to the east of Leighton Buzzard are first named at the end of the twelfth century, but were settled from earliest times. Eggington lies along the line of the ancient Thedeway, a road predating the Roman occupation. Clipstone was formerly bigger than Eggington, and once had its own chapel; at times they were taxed as separate hamlets.

Stanbridge to the south-east of the town took its name from the 'stone bridge' over the Ouzel stream at Stanbridgeford. It was granted by Henry I to his wife Matilda before 1118 and was later part of the dower lands of two queens. In 1215 its owner William de Gatesden was keeper of the King's gerfalcons (large hunting birds). It was more independent of Leighton Buzzard than the other hamlets in the Middle Ages, and in 1291 was described as having its own dovecot, fishponds and windmill.

Billington, on its hill south of Leighton Buzzard, was occupied in the Iron Age, before the Roman conquest, and is first named in 1196. Its two separate centres, now Great and Little Billington, were also known as East and West Billington, the former on top of the hill and the latter along the road to Slapton.

Linslade village grew up on the west bank of the Ouzel around St Mary's Church, in the north of the parish, with the hamlet of Southcott, the 'south cottages', developing later. The Thedeway formed its southern parish boundary as early as 966. Even earlier, in 906, the ford where Thedeway crossed the Ouzel at Yttingaford, was the site of a peace treaty between the King and the invading Danes. Today Tiddenfoot Leisure Centre recalls the spot.

The parish church of All Saints in Leighton Buzzard was the centre of religious life for the inhabitants of both the town and its hamlets. All baptisms, marriages and burials took place there at first. Then during the medieval period the villages began to build their own chapels of ease, somewhere to worship when the winter storms made journeys to town impossible. Baptisms and marriages came to be celebrated in the chapels but, except at Stanbridge, the right to bury the dead remained with All Saints' until the nineteenth century.

St Leonard's Church at Heath and Reach was built originally as a chapel for Heath House, and 'Heath chapelry' is documented in the sixteenth century. By contrast Eggington chapel, St Michael's, is mentioned much earlier, in 1273, and Clipstone too had a chapel, though this has now gone. Eggington was granted the right of burial in 1840 and marriage in 1843, though there are earlier records of marriages taking place in the village chapel. St John's Church at Stanbridge has an even earlier history, and in 1406 it was the first chapel to have burial rights. Billington chapel, also St Michael's, dates from the thirteenth century, and records show that some marriages were taking place there during the seventeenth century.

St Mary's was the parish church for Linslade and Southcott until the middle of the last century. It became famous for its holy well, and pilgrimages to Linslade were eventually banned by the Bishop of Lincoln in 1299. The village had its own market and fair in the thirteenth century, but it declined throughout the medieval period, until just the church, manor house and a few cottages were left.

By the time of the first national census in 1801 the population of Leighton Buzzard was close to 2,000, nearly ten times the figure for each of the villages, except Heath and Reach where 541 people lived. Linslade, where the Grand Junction Canal had just opened, also barely topped the 200 mark. However, the century brought great changes and Linslade started to grow. By 1831 the prosperity brought by the canal had doubled its population to 407, and thirty years later, following the building of the London to Birmingham railway, the figure stood at 1,500.

Leighton Buzzard grew more slowly, almost doubling its population by 1841, but the hamlets Stanbridge, Eggington and Billington did not achieve this before 1851, and Heath and Reach before 1871. The difference was the railway station built in 1838 which turned Linslade into a boom town. New roads were laid out around the railway, pubs and shops were built, and within a few years Linslade had developed another tourist trade to rival its medieval holy well – hunting. Frequent trains from London attracted the Rothschilds to Buckinghamshire where they built several great houses, and from the 1880s onwards their royal visitors were becoming a familiar sight. Two future monarchs, Edward VII and Edward VIII, hunted here.

In 1901 Linslade's population had reached 2,157, over ten times the figure for 1801. Leighton Buzzard stood at 6,331, slightly more than three times its 1801 figure. Heath and Reach was 1,062, Eggington was just 239, Stanbridge 342 and Billington 263. While Leighton and Linslade continued to grow the hamlets were shrinking in size.

In 1965 Linslade was taken into Bedfordshire and the two towns became Leighton-Linslade. The Tuesday and Saturday markets in Leighton High Street continue to be a focus for the outlying villages, just as they have been for a thousand years. And the railway station in Linslade serves the thousands of commuters who now live in the town.

CHAPTER ONE

LEIGHTON BUZZARD

All Saints' Church and the town's war memorial. All Saints' was first recorded in the thirteenth century. There was a fire here in 1985 which caused extensive damage. The Kempe windows survived as did the choir stalls, which were made late in the fourteenth century. The rood screen is about a hundred years later. The Jacobean pulpit was given to the town in 1638 by a member of the Wilkes family. The lectern, which is in the shape of an eagle, is nearly as old as the church itself; it has a chain for attaching a bible. The font is more than 700 years old so may have come from an older church, probably but not definitely on the same spot.

Hockliffe Street Baptist Chapel Sunday school teachers and officers, *c*. 1898. Hubert Janes is the third man from the left. The Hockliffe Street Baptist Chapel congregation has had several homes since it was formed as a splinter group of the Lake Street Baptists. In 1849 it moved into the Ebenezer Chapel in Hockliffe Street, next to the White House. One of the prime movers here was G.G. Aveline. By 1865 it was in the building vacated by the Wesleyan Methodists when their new chapel was built. The last move was to the present custom-built chapel in Hockliffe Street in September 1892.

2nd Leighton Buzzard Scout Group having their troop dinner in St Andrew's Church Room, 1921. By the 1860s the population of the town had grown and the non-conformists had built several chapels in the town. The Church of England responded by building a second church, and associated school and church rooms, at the North End of the town – St Andrew's. The church was consecrated on 11 July 1867. It could seat 600 worshippers. The local stone deteriorated so much that in 1964 the church was declared unsafe and demolished.

The Cedars School, High Street. The Cedars Secondary School at the junction of the High Street and Church Square opened in 1921. The first entrance exam was on 12 March: all students were accepted and the exam results were only used to sort the children into forms. There were forty-two boys and sixty-four girls divided between four classes, with ages from ten to eighteen. By 1924 numbers had risen to 205 pupils. In 1945 they stood at 400, and were to peak at 750 in 1973, after which the school moved to Mentmore Road as an upper school as part of the 'Comprehensive' reorganization of Bedfordshire schools. Now the building is home to Leighton Middle School, with children aged nine to thirteen years.

Cedars School Group. The first headmaster, Mr Fairbrother, is the gentleman wearing the mortar board. The boy sitting crosslegged second from the right is John Watling. The building had been the town house for members of the Bassett family until The Knolls and The Heath just off Plantation Road were built.

Watch the birdie, *c.* 1900. Ernest Edward Gilbert (1873–1942) is pictured here with his wife Sarah Jane (née Ayres, 1875–1956). He was the youngest of the four sons of James Gilbert, founder of Gilbert and Sons – one of the ironworks in the town. Ernest and Sarah were married on 30 December 1897 at All Saints', Leighton Buzzard. This picture was taken by William F. Piggott, a photographer in Leighton Buzzard and Winslow.

Beaudesert Boys' School, members of Wasps House, 1934. The Beaudesert Boys' School was built in 1893. In 1925 it was decided to divide the pupils into 'houses' to foster competitiveness and team spirit amongst the boys. At first there were two houses – Grasshoppers under Mr Muskett and Wasps with Mr Blake. Six months later a third house was formed, named Dragonfly, with Mr Young as house master.

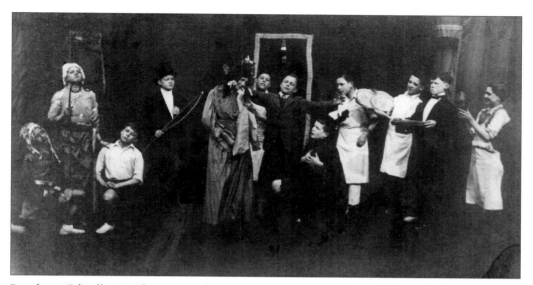

Beaudesert School's 1934 dramatic production, *Gertrude the Governess*. K.C. (Bob) Kiteley was co-author and took the title role. In the picture are Reg Dimmock, Ray Page, Les Horn, Eric Greeves, Bob Kiteley, Dennis Major, Fred Linney, Bill Heley, Derek Gilbert, Les Cosby, Hugh Aitken and George Rutland. In the first week in January 1959 the eleven to fifteen-year-old boys from this school and the older girls from the Mary Bassett School moved to a new building in Brooklands Drive. In 1975 Brooklands became a middle school for pupils aged nine to thirteen.

Also in 1934, Hugh Aitken and some of his friends at Beaudesert School gave a spirited performance as 'Aitken's Imps of Rhythm'. Their instruments were somewhat unusual, including combs, spoons and cymbals. This was one of the activities of the school dramatic society, run by Mr E.A. Muskett. Other societies in the school at that time were Fur and Feather, Natural History, Scientific, Photographic, Woodwork and Sports and Pastimes.

Fatstock Show, Church Square, post-1931. In the background is the showroom for the Leighton Buzzard Gas Company, opened at 2 High Street on Monday 19 January 1931. For the first month there was a 10 per cent discount on all orders for 'gas apparatus'. The building was replaced in the 1960s and here, until recently, you could still pay your gas bill, choose a new cooker, fire or central heating system. It now houses a charity shop for Sue Ryder.

Aerial view of the gas works, just prior to demolition. It ceased production in about 1960 and a few years later the town changed over to natural gas, one of the first towns in the country to do so. February 1835 saw the formation of the Leighton Buzzard Gas and Coke Company. By the end of 1835 thirty-two private houses and a few street lamps were being supplied with gas. The first plant was built on Billington Road, but by 1880 there was no room for more expansion, so 7 acres of land was purchased adjoining the Dunstable branch of the London and North Western Railway.

Vans from William Simmons in front of the Mill. Left to right: O.M. Harper, M. Harper, A. Lee, W. Scrivener. 'In Lestone there are two mills of thirty shillings.' This is how, in 1086, the mill in Leighton Buzzard was referred to in the Domesday Book. We believe the two mills were separate grinding mechanisms, one used for corn and the other probably for malt, both in the same building. The Simmons family connection with Leighton Buzzard dates from 1790 when Richard Simmons became a flour miller and corn merchant in the town. In 1874 Frederick Simmons bought Bellows Mill at Eaton Bray and took over the running of Leighton Mill. At Frederick's death in December 1891 his son William became the owner. William never married, so in 1929 A. Buckmaster and F. Tooley, his nephews, succeeded to the business. They kept the name of William Simmons to trade under and the brand name of Snowwis for their products.

Bonfire night, 1904. The warehouse of Tooley and Co. in Lake Street, now part of the Safeway complex, caught fire on the afternoon of 5 November. There are at least two versions of this picture. It appeared in local shops as a postcard within a few days of the event. There was one person hurt, a Mr Charles Gotzheim. The company used the local paper to inform their customers that the recent fire at their warehouse 'would not interfere with the delivery of forage'. Apparently 36,000 gallons of water were needed to fight the fire.

Mounted Officers, 2nd Battalion Bedfordshire Regiment, *c.* 1905. Left to right: Major E.D. Pickard-Cambridge, Lt.-Col. T. Hammond, Lt. Adjt. F.M. Bassett. Mr Bassett was a member of the local family who started the bank in Leighton Buzzard that later became Barclays in the High Street.

Leighton Buzzard detachment of 5th Battalion Beds & Herts Regiment, *c.* 1915. The soldier sixth from the left (middle row) is Harold Gilbert. The laundry in South Street can be seen in the background.

Harold Gilbert, aged about seventeen. At the time this picture was taken Harry was in the 3rd Volunteer Battalion Bedfordshire Regiment. The photograph was taken at the back of Brookfield Cottage, Plantation Road, the family home at the turn of the century. In about 1910 the 3rd Battalion merged to become the 5th Beds & Herts. Harold was the son of Albert Henry Gilbert. When Albert died, aged sixty, on 18 February 1927, he was a partner in Messrs Gilbert and Sons, Wheelwrights and Engineers, St Andrews Works.

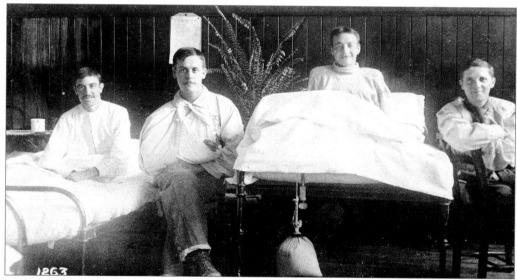

Casualties in the local hospital, c. 1916. The town was proud of its First World War record. At the end of the war a list of the names of over 1,400 men who served in the Army or Navy, with their war record, was published. Distinctions gained were DSO (2), OBE (1), MBE (1), DCM (6), Croix de Chevalier (1), Croix de Guerre (3), MM (13), Mentioned in Despatches (10). The local War Hospital Depot sent out no fewer than 82,756 articles, including 7,190 garments, 16,618 bandages, 52,296 dressings and 1,260 splints. There are 171 names of casualties from the First World War on the war memorial in Church Square.

The age of elegance, 1930s. Miss Gladys Mary Watling became a teacher working at Stanbridge School. Her mother was Florence, the youngest of three daughters of James Gilbert, who in 1897 married Ernest Alfred Watling, for many years the district rate collector. The Watling family had run a draper's shop at 66 North Street since at least 1890. In August 1931 this shop was taken over by Reginald Rivett from High Wycombe.

This picture shows the Gilbert Foundry in St Andrews Street. The business had started early in the nineteenth century in workshops near the present-day Peacock Market. In the picture are all four sons of James Gilbert (1839–92) and Emma his wife (1843–78), namely Albert, Frederick, William and Ernest, together with R. Gravestock and Messrs Major, Proctor and Johnson. This firm was one of two ironworks in Leighton Buzzard, the other being the Victoria Iron Works, Lake Street, which was demolished to make way for Safeways supermarket.

GIBBS & Co.,

FURNISHERS.

We have purchased for Cash the entire stock of a **MARGATE**

CHINA & GLASS MERCHANT

Over $6\frac{1}{4}$ tons.

We are now offering some choice

TEA AND DINNER SERVICES

at much below actual value.

Suitable for **XMAS PRESENTS.**

Gibbs & Co. 48 & 50 HIGH STREET

Leighton Buzzard

This advertisement for Gibbs & Company was on the back of a postcard view of Newgate Gap Steps, Cliftonville. The business stood on the site of today's Midland Bank, in the High Street. The London Joint City and Midland Bank came to the town in 1920 and built their premises at 48–50 High Street, where Gibbs and Co. house furnishers' shop had been. From January 1916 Ernest Frank Gibbs, of Torbay, Hockliffe Road, upholsterer, the grandson of James Gibbs (founder of the firm) served as a driver in the Royal Horse Artillery. Ernest fought in France and was demobilized in 1919.

A visit to the Marley Tile Company in Leighton Buzzard by the Institution of Municipal and County Engineers, 1933. In the picture are B.P. Janes and the surveyors of Hemel Hempstead, Luton and Hitchin, Messrs Murray-Smith, Pickering and Whittle. Marley Tile Co. Ltd came to the town in 1926, and grew from a small factory in a field to become the biggest producer of concrete roof tiles in the world. The firm is remembered locally by the housing estate Marley Fields, off Stanbridge Road, recently built on the site of the factory.

Aveline & Phillips removal van, Lake Street. George Gamaliel Aveline, upholsterer and complete house furnisher, in Lake Street, is mentioned in the 1876 directory. By 1894 the firm had become Aveline & Phillips, and they were still trading at 17–19 Lake Street in 1940. In 1914 the firm also had a branch in Linslade. Fire struck their cartsheds in Dudley Street on the last Friday in February that year but nobody was injured. They were even able to rescue some of the vans and stock stored there. The Ridgway & Pledger building with the triangular pediment can be seen on the left. It has classical features even though it was probably built in the reign of Queen Victoria.

Banners flying, Market Square, Whit Sunday, 1914. The bandsmen of the National Union of Railwaymen parade in their straw boaters. The march was in aid of the Widows' and Orphans' Fund. The marchers met in Station Road, Linslade, and marched to St Andrew's Church where a sermon was given by the Revd C.E. Douglas, at which he congratulated the Leighton Buzzard branch upon its growth in the past year. Included in the parade was Herbert Avery (holding the cornet) and the Drum and Fife Band of the Leighton Troop of Boy Scouts. At the cross short speeches were given by Councillor Dobbs of Neasden and Mr J.H. Carnhill of Willesden. The parade was organized by A.H. Holmes and J. Frost, secretary and treasurer, and the rest of the committee of the local branch of the NUR.

Walter Ebenezer Collett came to live in Leighton Buzzard in about 1894. He first set up shop in Vandyke Road from where he moved into Hockliffe Road. Almost immediately on his arrival in Leighton Buzzard he became a member of Hockliffe Street Baptist Church. He served as a church deacon for about sixty years, and just before he died on 10 February 1960, aged eighty-seven, was made an honorary life deacon.

W.E. Collett, plumbers, outside Walter Collett's shop in Hockliffe Road. Mr Collett is pictured with his wife Emily and their two sons Walter James and Albert George. When the Colletts traded from here (c. 1902 to 1908) it was known as 36 Hockliffe Road; the building still exists, numbered as 62 Hockliffe Road. After the Colletts moved closer to the centre of town the shop became a baker's and confectioner's run by Joseph William Peach. The Colletts moved from here, first to Hockliffe Street and in July 1959 to Dudley Street. After returning from service in the First World War, when he was awarded the Belgian Croix de Guerre, Walter James worked in the family business.

Miss Croxford making Bedfordshire pillow lace. Lace making was one of the crafts demonstrated when the Cedars School in Church Square was opened in 1921. The best-known member of the Croxford Family was Leonard, who was born in Heath and Reach in 1878. He was the eldest son of Thomas and Mary Croxford and had three brothers and four sisters. By 1910 he had opened a gents' outfitters at 44 North Street, and was living in Hartwell Grove. He was joined in business by his younger brother Frank who had served in the First World War, gaining the Military Medal. By 1924 Frank too was living in Hartwell Grove, next door to Leonard. By 1931, the year of their mother's death, in Heath and Reach, the North Street shop had expanded to occupy numbers 40–44. There have been other seemingly unrelated Croxfords trading in the town. Miss Agnes Elizabeth Croxford in 1910 was a dressmaker in Albany Road. In 1936 Mrs Violet Croxford was trading as a draper in Hockliffe Street.

Queues in the High Street: shoppers waiting outside Mr Bardell's fish shop during the Second World War. Note the bicycles, a favoured mode of transport when petrol was almost unobtainable. In the war everyone had ration books so that a fair share of available food could be distributed; even so queues formed. It was a time to catch up on all the latest gossip. Another queue would be for entrance to the cinema and a chance to escape to another world.

The star turn at the swimming gala, August Bank Holiday Monday, 1922. At this swimming carnival, held at 'Spinney Pit, Billington Crossing', the Swans, Miss F.M. Swan and Mr B.J. Swan, gave an exhibition of 'plain and fancy' swimming. This was the first annual gala of the Leighton Buzzard and District Swimming Club since their reformation. About 1,500 people attended: Leighton Buzzard Fire Brigade gave a display with their engine, using up to three hoses. On disconnecting one of the hoses they managed to soak some of the spectators.

Swimming Club Committee, 1922. The picture was taken on the diving board at Spinney Pool, Billington Road. The pool was a large sand pit which in 1921 had been filled with spring water to a depth of 30 ft. For a time from 1922 the National Amateur Swimming Association Championships were held here during the August Bank Holiday galas. It is said that the building of Battlesden water pumping station in 1937 caused the pool to lose water. By about 1942 it was too shallow for swimming, and in 1960 the land was purchased for development.

Population, 1801–1991

Year	1801	1811	1821	1831	1841	1851	1861	1871	1881	1891	1901	1911	1921	1931	1941[5]	1951	1961	1971	1981	1991
Billington	200	225	237	271	232	456	484	475	426	350	263	247	233	242	—	287	633	531	520	432
Eggington	206	223	302	348	396	431	439	375	274	268	239	236	240	243	—	228	301	284	1374[1]	266
Heath & Reach	541	586	726	784	856	925	953	1120	1075	1090	1062	1028	923	1022[2]	—	816	922	1103	1247	1316
Stanbridge	262	325	407	416	519	597	554	586	512	402	324	368	378	377	—	416	625	804	747	710
L.B. (town)	1963	2114	2749	3330	3965	4465	4330	5361	5991	—	—	—	—	—	—	—	—	—	—	—
L.B. (UDC)	—	—	—	—	—	—	—	—	6704[3]	6331	6782	6791	7030	—	9025[2]	11745	—	—	—	
Linslade	203	281	370	407	883	1309	1511	1680	1724	1982	2157	2262	2373	2433	—	3270	4130	—	—	—
Leighton-Linslade	—	—	—	—	—	—	—	—	—	—	—	—	—	—	—	—	—	20347[4]	29858[3]	31889

Notes to Population Table

1 Eggington, including some 300 houses brought into Eggington by a 1970s boundary change but transferred back to Leighton-Linslade in 1985.
2 Heath and Reach: part of the parish transferred to Leighton Buzzard Urban District Council in 1933.
3 Leighton Buzzard: the township became an Urban District in 1891, reverting to the status of a town council in 1974.
4 Leighton-Linslade: from 1965 the figures include Linslade, which was formerly in Buckinghamshire.
5 No census taken during the war.

Leighton Buzzard Regnal Hockey Club, 1930/1. Peter Quick, for many years the town clerk, is the central seated figure. It was on 29 June 1992 that Mr Quick announced his retirement after forty-two years of service to the town. He had also acted as local registrar of births, deaths and marriages, and was a magistrate and school governor for many years.

Leighton Buzzard Rugby Football club, 1949/50. The club was formed on 27 June 1934, and their first match was on 6 October 1934. It was played on their home ground off Billington Road against an Aylesbury team. The home team won by 11 points to 6. By their second season the club membership stood at forty-two and they were using a pitch in Bell Close. However, they had to disband for the duration of the war, reforming in 1948/9. Despite some setbacks 1958 saw them playing on a pitch at Clipstone Meadow. The club stayed here until the land was sold for houses. The club was then able to buy the present ground, called Wrights Meadow, on the Stanbridge Road. Matches started here in the 1974/5 season. By this date the club was large enough to field four teams.

The Merry Mascots, 1913. At the beginning of April 1913 the local paper reported: 'This popular concert party delighted the inmates at the Workhouse with several humorous and other songs and a sketch entitled The Wrong Flat.' The troupe performed the same sketch a month later in the Corn Exchange as part of a concert to raise funds for themselves. The Mascots had 'an extensive repertoire of well-chosen songs and an abundance of comic and one or two rag-time numbers'. In the picture are Percy Dimmock, Alfred Westmancote, Connie Kirby, Elsie Reeve, Ronald Walker, Chrissie McBane, Albert Price, Reginald Cornish and Jack Brotherton.

Leighton, Dunstable, Luton railway line crossing the Billington Road, 1917. The level crossing gates have gone and the signals too. There is now a line of pylons on the skyline, with Pratts Quarry entrance on the left near where they cross the road. The LNWR branch railway from Leighton Buzzard via Dunstable to Luton opened on 1 June 1848. This was just ten years after the opening of the main line through Linslade. The line closed to through goods trains on 1 January 1966. Its death knell was sounded when the Rugby Cement Company built a pipeline to carry slurried chalk from its quarries at Totternhoe and Kensworth to Southam. Part of the line between Linslade and Grovebury Sidings remained operative for a year or two longer, and then the rest of the track was removed.

Frank Griffin's shop, now numbered 58–62 Hockliffe Street. Frank Griffin opened as a wireless dealer here at 40 Hockliffe Street in about 1928. He stocked Marconiphone and Osram Music Magnet sets which you could have for a seven-day home trial. The former cost £18 18s, or £1 13s down and twelve monthly payments of £1 10s 6d. By 1930 he was also selling the 'Ariel Bicycle'. When the shop was modernized a mosaic plaque of a red griffin was mounted on the front above the doorway. The plaque is still there even though the shop now houses ComputaScene.

Victoria Nurseries, which was first mentioned in South Street in 1898 when it was run by Charles Heinrich Hatton, who was described as a florist, nurseryman and seedsman. By 1914 the business was in the hands of George Clarke. It closed in 1932 when the house, land and greenhouses were sold; the house is still standing. George Clarke also had premises in Heath Road, from where he traded as a florist from about 1910 until after 1940. In a directory for 1894 there are six nurserymen and/or market gardeners in the town, including John Samuel Birdsey at 49 Hockliffe Street: he had the colourful occupation of 'onion, potato and cucumber grower'.

Mr Page, 1894. William Sharp Page died on Sunday 29 October 1899 at his home The Elms, 33 High Street, aged sixty-nine. He was born in the town on 5 June 1830, the eldest of two sons of Charles Page. On leaving school William worked for a short time as a silversmith and ironmonger at the family shop in the High Street. Mr Page senior retired in 1856, at which time William Sharp Page seems to have retired from trade as well. In 1865 he helped form a Freehold Land Society, which in 1867 bought the land to develop Ashwell Street, Grove Road and Edward Street. Later the group was involved in the building of Albany Road, George Street and Woburn Terrace. Mr Page was also director of the Leighton Gas Company, and was active in many good causes in the town.

Page's Almshouses. These six almshouses in Church Street were built in 1903 in the quarry from which the material to build St Andrew's Church had been excavated. In his will W.S. Page left 'two closes of freehold land situated at Stonhill containing about 15 acres to be used as a public recreation ground or park for the use of the inhabitants of Leighton Buzzard, and to be called Page's Park'. He also left £1,200 to purchase freehold land at Leighton Buzzard for six almshouses for two married couples, two single men and two widows or spinsters, plus money for the upkeep of the buildings.

Boys playing in Grove Road. The Freehold Land Society began the development of Grove Road in 1867. By 1876 the road's residents included Mr George S.D. Harris, surgeon, and, at Grove House, the Ashdown brothers who had the brewery just off the High Street. By 1880 the road had been extensively developed with high-class houses for the businessmen from the town who had previously lived 'over the shop'.

Leighton Buzzard Board of Guardians, Wing Rural District Council, Eaton Bray Rural District Council, members and officials. Front row, left to right: M. Jennings, J.D. Britten, R. Purrett, A.A. Buckmaster, P. Hart, C. Buckmaster, P. Blake (Assistant Clerk), Rev. T. Harvey, Second row: W.G. Holloway, G.C. Thomas, Dr Lewis Worts (Medical Officer), A. Collyer, V. Woodman, A. Harrowell, J.W. Heley, C.H.G. Harrison, C.W.B. Calcott (Clerk), Bryan Walsh, J. Sharratt, G. Batchelar. Third row: J.T. Till (Relieving Officer), C. Rogers, W.F. Broom (Surveyor to Eaton Bray Rural District), D. Eames, J.J. Brooke, J.J.R. Adams, F.G. Pratt, J. Inwards, J. Stanbridge, C.H. Swaffield (Master). Fourth row: W. Woodhouse, J.H. Hawkins, M.G. Gurney (Surveyor to Wing Rural District), L. Newton, J. Phillips Corners. Lower: Dr J. Waugh (Medical Officer for Hockliffe District), Joseph Pratt, G. Chapman, G. Garside. Upper: Dr J.G. Durran (Medical Officer to Eaton Bray District), Dr P. Stedman (Medical Officer to Wing District), H.M. Roberts, B.F.J. Gates, The duties and powers of these three bodies were later taken over by new district councils under local government reorganization.

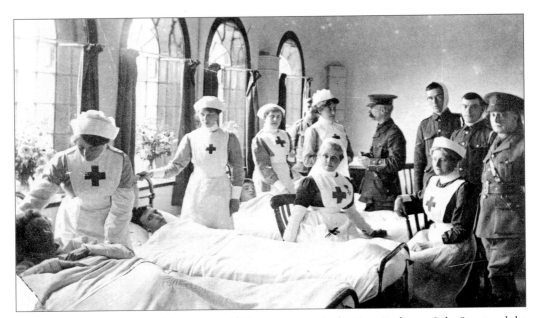

Wards for nursing casualties of the First World War were set up in the Corn Exchange, Lake Street and the Union Workhouse in Grovebury Road. The local scout movement was kept alive during this period by Mr and Mrs Bowden Purchase, helped by Nurse Eileen Ericson, seen here seated in the centre. Nurse Ericson, working from her home in Church Street, encouraged the older scouts to learn first aid so that they could help with the wounded.

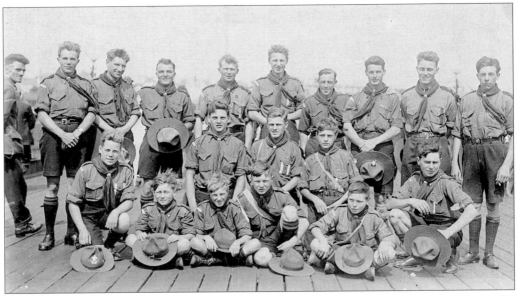

The Leighton Buzzard scout troop, The Buzzards, at Clacton for their annual camp in either 1927 or 1928. Fred Rowe (d. 1931) was made the first scout master of the troop on 20 July 1909. Music formed an important activity for the scouts and in 1913 Mr Holmes started a drum and fife band. Later Fred Groom (d. 1997) formed the Brass and Reed Band, which gave its first performance to the inmates of the Union Workhouse on 13 February 1923.

The foundation stone of the headquarters for the local scouts was laid in Grovebury Road by Mrs Wallace on 26 February 1938. The Wallace family ran a horticultural nursery at Eaton Bray growing carnations. Presenting the silver trowel is Cub Ronald Sanders. Also present are Mr S. Morris (chairman of the building committee), Mr M.C. Clifford (secretary), Mr Howard Spensley (County Commissioner), Revd E. Scott (District Commissioner) and Dr C.M. Cowper (Chairman of Leighton Buzzard Boy Scouts Association).

Opening of the Scout Headquarters by Mr Wallace, known as 'Squire', 6 June 1938. Alan Rowe, son of the late Mr Fred Rowe, presented Thanks Badges to all members of the Building Committee. The Revd C. Douglas formed the first Scout Group in the town in 1909 with six boys. This was just a year after Baden Powell had founded the movement. Tom Lawson joined the movement in 1923, serving in various capacities until his retirement, on 22 April 1981. Twenty scouts and officers served in the First World War; ten of them never came back.

The White House. This building now houses the Town Council. It was built in the middle of the last century in an Italianate style for Charles Ridgway, who had a draper's shop in Lake Street. At first it was known as The Villa but in about 1890 the then resident Robert Tindall changed the name to The White House. By 1914 the Garside family were living there. The Garsides were in the sand trade in the district. On 19 December 1978 the local paper reported the takeover of George Garside (Sand) Ltd, at which time they had five quarries and production plants in the district, employing thirty-six people.

Beechcroft School, Hockliffe Street. We first find direct reference to this property in 1910 when Robert William Douglas was living there. By 1914 it had become a girls' school, Beechcroft, run by Miss Millicent Draper. In about 1940 Miss E.N. James was appointed as its principal. The building remains, Delta House, but the gardens have made way for a roundabout. It was here on 9 July 1931 that a garden fête was held to start the building fund for the Scout Headquarters in Grovebury Road.

CHAPTER TWO

LINSLADE

The church at Old Linslade, dedicated to St Mary, was built in 1166 by the de Beauchamp family, who had been given the Manor of Linslade by William the Conqueror following his victory at Hastings in 1066. The little church was famous in the Middle Ages for the healing properties of its nearby Holy Well, until in 1299 the Bishop of Lincoln threatened the many pilgrims who flocked there with excommunication. This photograph from the fields to the south was taken in 1917.

A sketch of the old parish church by Frederick Gurney, drawn on 16 July 1919. The tower is fifteenth-century but the chancel and nave retain features from the original early medieval building. Gurney came from a local family and spent much of his time delving into the history of the village. He identified some graffiti inside the church: ' . . . a Jesu helpe', perhaps an echo of the Black Death in 1349.

St Mary's seen from the churchyard on the north side. The old north door can be seen in this late nineteenth-century photograph. It was blocked up during restoration of the church. Rendering still covers the church walls, which dates the photograph to the period before the major restoration of 1899, paid for by Henry Finch, a wealthy local businessman.

This interior photograph of St Mary's clearly shows the early chancel arch, which dates from the twelfth century. The chancel has a sedilia — seating for the priest — and the remains of what may have been the rood altar to the left of the arch. It also has an unusual seat next to the chancel arch. Among the monuments is a brass from the early sixteenth century depicting a merchant and his three wives with twelve children. The massive stone font with its mythical beasts dates from the twelfth century.

With the building of the railway through Linslade in 1838 a new town sprang up around the station, and the New Road was laid out across the green fields to connect the railway with Leighton Buzzard. St Mary's was too small and too distant for new Linslade and in 1849 St Barnabas's Church was built across the meadow from the station. This photograph was taken in 1903 and shows sheep grazing on what is now the Recreation Ground.

An interior photograph of the solidly splendid Victorian church. St Barnabas's was built in the heart of the new town, to accommodate four times as many worshippers as St Mary's. Among its treasures is a window by William Morris. Its bells ring out across the Recreation Ground to the station, welcoming weary commuters home.

The National school next to the new church was also built in 1849. During the nineteenth century Linslade had many private academies catering for the middle classes of the London suburbs who wished to send their children away to school in the country. The railway link made Linslade an ideal centre. The old school building survives as St Barnabas's Church Hall, and is busy with everything from jumble sales and dog training classes to meetings of the University of the Third Age.

A new board school was built in Leopold Road, and today is one of the town's lower schools. This staff photograph was taken in 1965, when the playground overlooked green fields. Back row, left to right: Mrs Sisley, Mrs B. Ellis, Mr J. Wigley, Mr D. Jury, Mr J. Mack, Mrs Val Scott. Middle row: Mrs J. Pedlow, Miss J. Collings, Mrs J. Loveday (school secretary), Mr R. Loveday (school headmaster), Mr Alan Scott, Miss I. Brown, Mrs I. Brazier. Front row: Miss M. Rush, Miss Stewart.

Leopold Road was almost certainly named after Leopold de Rothschild, who lived at nearby Ascott House and owned much of Southcott. This staff photograph from Leopold Road School was taken in 1967. Back row, left to right: Mrs I. Brazier. Miss I. Brown, Mrs M. Barraclough, Mr J. Mack, Mr S. Williams, Mr J. Wigley, Mr Alan Scott, Mr D. Jury, Mrs B. Ellis, Mrs M. Willis, Mrs Sisley. Front row: Mrs J. Pedlow, Mrs V. Romer, Mrs J. Loveday, Mr R. Loveday, Miss J. Collings, Mrs Maloney, Mrs Wright.

Tooley's Mill, in Old Road close to the canal, probably dates from the early part of the nineteenth century. A.W. Tooley and Son, corn and coal merchants, operated from there before the First World War. The mill in Old Road still survives, though the canal trade is now restricted to holiday traffic. This photograph from the 1950s shows a charity stall in the car park of the Bedford Arms, opposite the mill.

Harry Hunt's motor repair shop in what is now the car park of the Bedford Arms pub. In 1918 he was advertising the latest Ford touring car for £260. The car inside the garage on the left is the Standard that belonged to Dr Langley of Wing; his gardener Mr Rose had dropped a wing nut into the gearbox while greasing it and left it there. Result: wrecked gears and a visit to Harry Hunt's! The hydrant in front of the car supplied water for steam engines and water carts. The mechanics standing on the right are, left to right, Dennis 'Speedy' Turney, Percival Frederick 'Mickey' Martin, Ernest Chandler and Edwin Jessie 'Ted' Martin.

At 11 a.m. on Thursday 11 November 1920 Linslade paid tribute to its sons who had fallen in the First World War, with the unveiling of a memorial cross in what was then called Linslade Square, and is now the traffic-light festooned junction of the Wing and Old Roads. Dr Johnstone Harris, a well-loved local doctor and chairman of the Urban District Council, paid tribute to their memory in a simple speech touched with emotion. As the local paper noted, the community numbered less than 3,000 and the men who fell were known to most of the inhabitants – and particularly to Dr Harris who had known them as children.

This photograph of the cross is from the other direction and shows Leighton Road and Bridge Street crossing the canal and river bridges into Leighton Buzzard. The cross is 17 ft high and cost £300, being made by local stonemason Mr Thomas Yirrell. In 1955 it was removed to the Memorial Gardens in Mentmore Road, and those who died on active service in the Second World War are also remembered here.

Bridge Street, looking towards Linslade, in 1905 before the petrol stations and supermarkets moved in, and when traffic meant the occasional horse and cart. Only one of the elegant houses on the right survives today.

The same view twenty years later with the Grand Cinema on the right, the town's first purpose-built cinema. It was built by Thomas Yirrell in 1922 and could seat 500 people. When it re-opened in 1930 for 'talkies' it boasted carpeting throughout, and a cycle shed under lock and key for out-of-town patrons!

Thomas Brantom, born in 1848, was the founder of Brantom's forage, corn, coal and seed merchants who operated from Grant's Wharf on the canal. This photograph was taken just before his early death in 1892.

The wharf is today known as Brantom's Wharf, and local people will remember the Brantom's shops in North Street and the High Street. The elegant Grand Union House, just out of the photograph to the left, has recently been renovated, and a furnishing store now operates from Brantom's building seen here.

The canal frozen over, 1950s. The bridge that carried the towpath over the basin of Grant's or Brantom's Wharf can be seen. It was saved by public pressure when the site was redeveloped, but the basin is now dry and has become an office car park.

A typical canal narrow boat which used to transport the sand and coal, or corn and seed. Today they make popular floating holiday homes, and are busy throughout the summer months with day trippers and special outings, as seen in this photograph from the 1950s.

The Grand Junction Canal opened through Linslade in May 1800, and wharves grew up where it intersected roads. Whiting (Totternhoe chalk pulverized for use in whitewashing), coal, seed, corn and fruit from local orchards were all transported by narrow boat south to London and north to Birmingham. This narrow boat was photographed near the main town bridge in the 1950s.

Whichello's Wharf, opposite Morgan's Carriage Works on the canal north of the town bridge. It had originally been called Osborn's Wharf, and was also known as Chelsea Wharf. By 1861 Stephen Henry Whichello, a woolstapler from Oxfordshire, was in business there. He later built The Elms, an impressive house in Stoke Road backing on to the Wharf. Today it is a small housing estate.

Morgan's carriage works came to the canalside site in Linslade in the late 1880s, and made everything from horse-drawn carriages to motor cars and aeroplanes, employing 800 local people. Several spectacular fires gutted the works, including one in 1901 when carriages being prepared for the coronation of Edward VII were destroyed. During the First World War they made Vimy bombers, wheeling the bodies through the town, up Lake Street and Billington Road to Scott's Field, where the wings were fitted and members of the Royal Flying Corps flew them away.

Much of the bodywork and wings of the Vimy was made from canvas or linen, and seamstresses were employed at the works to sew the fabric. Mrs Violet Kate Guess worked for Morgan's before her marriage in 1923, and is seen in the previous photograph sitting in the front row. Here she is with her new baby son Eric in the late summer of 1924, with his great grandmother Mrs Jane Chamberlain (centre) and his grandmother Mrs Catherine Hopkins (right).

Inside Morgan's workshops during the First World War, making Vimy aeroplanes. At the end of the war the government of the day cancelled their aircraft contracts and 500 men were thrown out of work. But Morgan's soon resumed production of the motor car. The site is now covered by supermarkets and car parks.

George Chandler's baker's shop on the corner of Wing Road and Church Road, at the end of the last century. He was the son of an agricultural labourer from Northall and married the daughter of the Standbridge plait dealer and baker Jesse Goodman. He opened the bakery with his young wife soon after their marriage in 1879.

By the late 1890s George Chandler was also a coal and coke merchant operating from Charity Wharf, on the Grand Union Canal, opposite his shop. He lived with his family of three sons and two daughters over the shop. This later photograph shows that he transferred his coal and coke depot to Railway Wharf on the canal, further south, between 1900 and 1906.

The shop in the 1920s. George Chandler died in 1937 and the business passed to his second son Frederick, who in 1939 was listed in the directories as a coal merchant. In recent years the shop has become the home of Linslade Youth Club, but most people will know it as the local polling station at election time.

Across the Wing Road from Chandler's bakery shop stood Monson's Brewery, purpose-built in the early years of this century. The company soon went bankrupt and by 1910 the premises were occupied, in extreme contrast, by the Society of the Faith, who published religious books. The Faith Press remained there until the 1960s. Today the building houses a motor bike shop.

Yirrell's butcher's shop at 7–9 Old Road, with William Yirrell in the doorway, 1885. William was the youngest son of William Yirrell of Leighton Buzzard, and his three elder brothers – Samuel, Charles and Henry – all had shops in Leighton.

Left :   William Yirrell, Senior.
            1861 to 1938.

Right :   William Yirrell, Junior.
            1884 to 1962.

Below :   The present owner,
            W. B. A. Yirrell, who
            was born in 1927.

William Yirrell senior (left) married Esther Austin of Ambrosden and their house adjoining the shop is still called Ambrosden House. Their son William junior (right) was born here in the summer of 1884 while his father was haymaking in Bridge Meadows. The Yirrell family still run the butcher's shop, which they supply from their three local farms.

At the beginning of the Second World War Coty's established a factory at the Rothschild Stud Farm in Southcott to make reconnaissance and pathfinder flares. The larger pathfinder flares needed a parachute attachment, and local women were employed checking and folding the parachutes. Southcott House was turned into their offices, and the work was done in prefabs in the fields close to the stables. Another field was used to test the gunpowder for the flares, and local children prized the flares which floated down on test days. Among the workers was Yvonne de Rothschild, wife of Anthony and mother of Evelyn de Rothschild, the present owner of the Stud. In this photograph, taken in June 1945 as the war ended, can be seen (among others): Thelma Seed, Miss Bates, Margaret Rickard, Mrs Andrews, Iris Sage, Mrs Palmer, Joan Hall, Edith Thorpe, Margaret Randall, Harry Corkett, Georgina Dimmock, Mr and Mrs Albert Dimmock, Olive Farmborough and Ray Probert.

The final end of the Second World War was marked by celebrations and parties all over Linslade. In this photograph fifty children from Springfield Road, Southcourt Road, Southcourt Avenue, Rock Lane and Leopold Road have sat down to tea at a party in Leopold Road. Later, sports were held in a meadow lent by Mrs Rawle of Southcourt Farm, with pony rides and a firework display.

The Victory Tea for Soulbury Road children was held on the service road in front of the council houses, and despite rationing seventy children sat down to loaded tables. Every child went home with an orange and a small gift. The Old Road party included a motor tour of Wing airport to watch the planes landing, and Rothschild Road and Stoke road children were given a film show in the garage of Flaxton House. This photograph shows the Ashburnham Crescent party, with children from Wing Road and Mentmore Road.

The Forster Institute at 1 Waterloo Road was built to replace the Parish Reading Rooms in New Road. On 11 June 1890 the foundation stone was laid by Mrs C.M. Forster, in memory of her late husband. Costing just over £1,000 and designed by local architect Mr J.T. Lawrence, the Institute had a spacious lecture hall, with a similarly sized room below for 'a reading and smoking room . . . utilised also for games'.

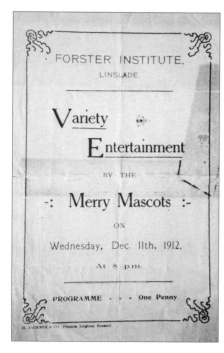

Mrs Forster remarried, becoming Mrs Simpson, and lived for many years in Linslade Villa in Church Road. The Institute was described at the time of her death in 1911 as 'an excellent hall . . . of inestimable benefit to parish work'. It was the venue for everything from 'smoking concerts' for the Conservative and Unionist Association and exhibitions on missionary work in China to political meetings at election time and entertainments. The Merry Mascots featured on this programme of 1912 are pictured on p. 26.

This photograph from the turn of the century belonged to the Chandler family who ran the bakery in Wing Road. We don't know exactly what the event was, but from the bunting and flags it was probably part of local celebrations of the Queen's Diamond Jubilee in 1897. Today the Forster Institute is still serving the people of Linslade; it is the meeting place for many local societies and is also used for drama and dance classes, and playgroups.

This postcard, dated 9 October 1907, shows the Grove Isolation Hospital, which was tucked in a wedge of land between the railway and the road to Ledburn, just on the parish boundary with Grove. It provided nursing care for diphtheria and typhoid cases in the district, its lonely position helping to stem the spread of disease. Nurse Pound, who sent the postcard, writes: 'am taking holiday duty here for Matron for one month. Fearfully busy – 9 patients.' During the 1960s the hospital provided physiotherapy services, but was finally demolished in the 1980s when the town bypass was built over the site.

The Manor House at Linslade seen from the tower of nearby St Mary's Church. There has probably been a house on this site for at least 600 years, though most of the present house dates from the eighteenth century. Stone cellars and medieval tiles found during building work give glimpses of its past. From the sixteenth century the Manor was the home of the Corbet family, who were Lords of the Manor. Linslade was often left to the widow as a dower property, and in 1679 Sarah, widow of Sir Vincent Corbet, was created Viscountess Lynchlade in recognition of her husband's support of Charles I during the Civil War.

The oldest part of the present house is probably the kitchen range at the back, and it was from here that the stone plaque of a raven with the latin motto 'Deus Pascit Corvos' was taken. There was also said to be a datestone of 1666. The motto translates as 'God Feeds the Raven', the raven or crow being part of the heraldic arms of the Corbet family, and – coming from the old French word for crow, 'corbie' – being a play on their name.

The Martins, an exotic black and white house in the Chinese style, was built on the canal side by Gordon Cale Thomas, engineer to the Grand Junction Canal Company, at the end of the nineteenth century. Among its charms were seven bedrooms with balconies overlooking the Ouzel valley and the canal, three reception rooms plus a billiard room, and a tennis lawn sunk below ground level to form a skating rink in winter. In the summer local children enjoyed Sunday School teas in the gardens.

Mr Thomas did not enjoy his lovely home for long; in May 1916 he was charged with embezzlement at Bow Street Police Court. The house and extensive grounds were put up for sale at £3,300, to include both the tennis and croquet lawns, the kitchen garden, and two paddocks. After the Second World War it was converted into flats, and was burnt down and demolished in 1971. Today only the Lodge, seen here, remains.

Something of the grandeur of the house is echoed in this attractive folly, a small stone tower which still stands at the entrance to the original drive.

A close-up of the stone dolphin which decorates the folly. Nearby are the remains of what is commonly believed to be the ice house of The Martins. Today The Martins is a small estate of expensive canal-side houses.

The Gables, off the Wing Road, was another of Linslade's grand Victorian houses, whose name, like The Martins, is now chiefly remembered in the housing estate which stands on its site. It was built in the 1880s by Henry Finch, a wealthy London businessman, who enjoyed the hunting in Buckinghamshire and made Linslade his country home. This aerial photograph shows the handsome gates on to Waterloo Road.

Henry Finch was the first Chairman of Linslade Urban Council. His generosity to Linslade was unbounded. In 1889 he marked the marriage of his only child, Louisa Kate, with the gift of an organ to St Barnabas's Church, where the wedding took place. He then paid for the complete restoration of the medieval parish church of St Mary's to mark Queen Victoria's Diamond Jubilee in 1897. Lastly he bought the fields near the railway station at full market value – they were sold as building land – and presented them to the village for a Recreation Ground.

With the death of Henry Finch in 1910, The Gables became the home of his widow Lavinia, and then his daughter and her husband, Dr Sidney Roberts, and their family. After the war it became a girls' school, which closed in 1969. Today only the magnificent billiard room survives, seen above in its original splendour, together with some windows from the house, decorated in coloured glass with finches. When the house was demolished to build the new estate the single-storey wing containing the billiard room was retained.

CHAPTER THREE

HEATH & REACH

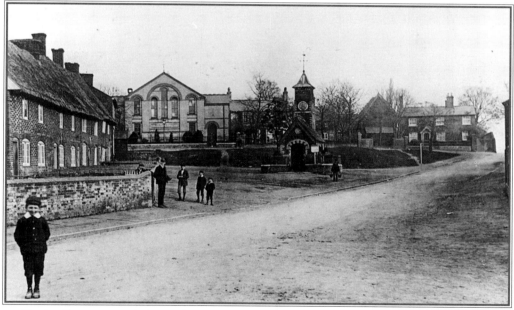

Heath village green at the heart of the old village. The road up the hill from Leighton Buzzard passes through on its way to Reach and then on to Watling Street. It is unrecognizable as today's Leighton Road with its constant traffic of sand lorries. The well on the green was sunk in 1859 and supplied water to the village, until mains water was laid on in the 1930s. The picturesque well house, with a pump, and the clock tower were built by public subscription, and opened on 12 May 1873. Iron's Row is on the left, with the Wesleyan Methodist Chapel looming over the Green.

Lane's End where it faces on to the Green, with pretty, thatched cottages that were once home to the poorest families in the village. The 1891 census records seventeen inhabited homes in Lane's End, many of them with only four rooms. Overcrowding was just one of the miseries endured by poor rural families at the end of the last century; Richard Evans, a forty-nine-year-old agricultural labourer, lived in one small cottage with his wife and seven children.

This thatched cottage on the Lane has now been demolished. In 1841 there were fourteen dwellings along Lane's End, with seventy-two people living in them. Over half were children, and apart from one farmer and one washerwoman everyone else was employed as either a straw plaiter, if female, or an agricultural labourer.

Heath Green looking towards Leighton Buzzard, with the Duke's Head pub on the left. An old thatched building, the Duke's Head stands back from the roadway. It is listed in the 1822 alehouse licences, but its history probably stretches back into the eighteenth century. During much of the nineteenth century Thomas Dancer ran the pub, and in 1894 it advertised 'good stabling and traps to and from the station'.

Opposite the Duke's Head a group of soldiers pose for the camera in the early years of this century. They are outside 6 Heath Green, which was then one of the village bakeries. It was run by Richard Kirby and in the doorway stand Mr and Mrs Williams. In 1924 the village had a post office, a draper's, a hardware shop, two butchers, a dairy, two other bakers, two boot repairers, and four general shops.

St Leonard's Church was originally the chapel of ease to Heath Manor house, which stands opposite. In 1705 Elizabeth, the daughter and heir of Richard Wigg of Heath Manor, and wife of John Frank, gave 'her chapel' and its chancel to the 'inhabitants of the hamlet of Heath and Reach'. It was largely rebuilt in the nineteenth century, the tower now being all that remains of the old chapel.

Heath Manor was described in 1666 as 'newly built', though recent carbon dating has given a date of 1460 to some of its timbering. It was advertised for rent at £26 per annum, and included 'garrets etc, 24 rooms, six wainscotted including the Studdye'. The valuation also said that the cost of building the house, chapel and almshouse was £2,000. A little later it was included in a description of the Leighton estates of Mr Wells and more details emerged: 'a mansion house with seven lower rooms, also cellars, two butteries, two studies, two kitchens, a wainscotted hall, two wainscotted parlours, ten chambers, three stables, a coachhouse, barn, an orchard and two gardens.'

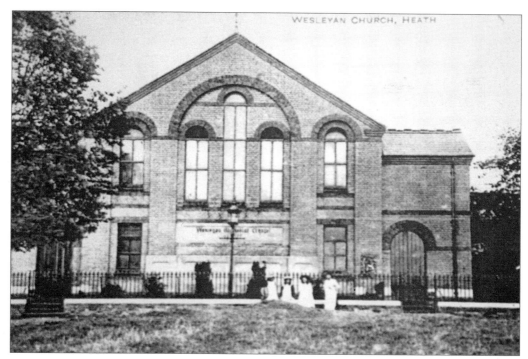

The Wesleyan Methodist Chapel now on Heath Green was built in 1877, and replaced an earlier chapel constructed in 1822. In the mid-nineteenth century between two and three hundred villagers attended the chapel. There was also a Primitive Methodist chapel in Woburn Road — now an antiques shop — and a Baptist chapel in the village.

A school outing to Heath Manor gardens in 1913, at the invitation of the Misses Mary, Annie and Kate Blewitt. In 1906 their brother Colonel Charles Turner Blewitt of the Royal Field Artillery had been killed while hunting locally. His body was brought back to Heath House, and a funeral with full military honours took place.

The first National School at Heath and Reach was built on the corner of Birds Hill and the old Linslade Road in 1846. It served the children of both hamlets. This photograph from 1896 shows the boys and girls outside the school.

The village directory for 1853 states that Frederick White was the schoolmaster and that the average attendance was forty-five. Since there were two plait dealers resident in the village, many children would have attended straw plait schools, where they could earn a few pence as well as – possibly – learning to read and write. This photograph shows the schoolchildren in 1898, by which time the school had been rebuilt, and an infants' classroom added. Attendance was now ninety-six, plus ninety infants.

This photograph, with the girls in their white pinafores, shows the schoolmaster Mr W. Taylor on the far right, and the schoolmistress Mrs Taylor, formerly Hilda Brantom, on the left. The old school was demolished in the 1990s and a new school built in Thrift Road. The old school site is now housing.

Bruce was the pet dog of Miss Brown, schoolmistress at Heath during the First World War. This photograph was the birthday card she sent to one of her pupils, eight-year-old Alice Stone, and it says on the back: 'With every good wish for a bright and happy birthday.' Eighty years later Alice remembered that Bruce came into class every day, sitting under Miss Brown's desk.

Woburn Road at Reach at the turn of the century with children playing in the empty road, opposite the baker's shop. Matthew Robinson's bakery in the 1920s delivered bread by horse and cart as far as Great Brickhill. Mr Arthur Shales, who had lived all his life in the village, working at the sandpits, remembers the smell of the new bread and Mrs Robinson in her white apron. Other shops along this stretch of road were Croxford's haberdashers, a butcher and a rag and bone merchant.

The schoolchildren of Heath and Reach celebrate May Day in the school playground, 1 May 1910. The tradition of bringing in the May – celebrating the coming of summer – dates back to the Middle Ages and probably originated as a pagan festival. During the late nineteenth century the custom was taken over by village schools, and prizes were given and teas arranged for the children. Today's May Day holiday, when 'workers of the world unite', has no connection with this ancient feast day.

An old and faded photograph showing Reeve's smithy at Reach Green, near the present Cockhorse Pub. Thomas Reeve, the blacksmith, was forty-two in the 1891 census and lived here with his wife Betsy and four children. His father, also Thomas Reeve, had kept the Cock beershop in 1851, when this part of Woburn Road was known as Rogues Row. The elder Thomas was also manager at the sandpits, and the Cock was a favourite pub of the sandworkers.

The Red Lion at Reach, one of the village's large popular pubs, is recorded in 1780, when William Bates, a victualler, insured his dwelling house 'known as the Red Lion' for £65. It was then described as built from brick and timber, panelled with brick and plaster, and thatched. This photograph from 1929 shows the new building we know today, with publican Frederick Stone and his daughter Alice standing outside.

Throughout the nineteenth century the Belgrove family, who were also butchers, ran the Red Lion. By 1914 Frederick Stone, who was also the village carrier, owned the pub. In 1913 he had brought the first motor vehicle to the village, a Ford taxi. This old (and poor-quality) photograph shows his carts outside the pub.

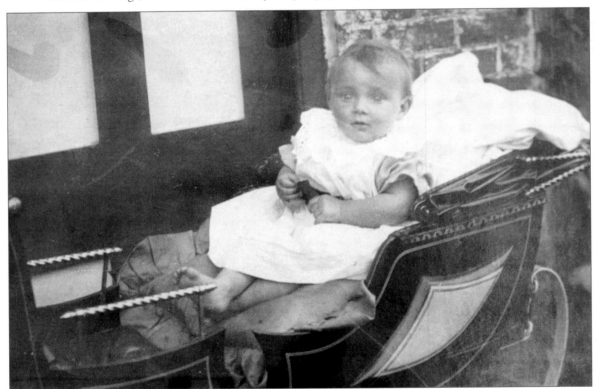

His daughter Alice Vera Stone was born in 1907, and this photograph of her in her pram was taken by a travelling photographer outside one of the old cottages in Maltings Lane, near to present-day Thrift Road.

Alice and her dog Lark in June 1908, sitting on her father's wagon in Wing Road, Linslade. The strange object on the back is not an early moon rocket, but a new cowl for St Leonard's Church chimney, which Mr Stone had just collected from the railway station at Linslade. In the background can be seen George Chandler's grocery shop on the corner of Church Road and Wing Road. Alice became Mrs Freeman and lived on into the 1990s in Heath and Reach, and was a popular visitor at the village school with her stories of old village life.

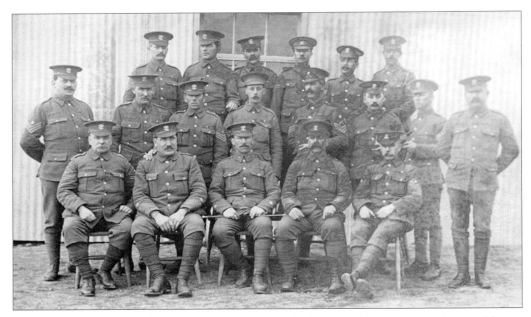

A group of soldiers billetted in Heath and Reach during the First World War. Nicknamed 'The Old Dug-Outs', they are in the field behind the Red Lion, in front of the corrugated iron shed which provided their quarters. The village war memorial in the churchyard records the names of thirty-eight men and one woman who lost their lives on active service during the First World War.

The Grange in Woburn Road, Reach, opposite the Red Lion, was the home of David Thomas Willis — or Lawyer Willis as he was known to the locals, a member of the Leighton Buzzard legal family. He built the thirteen-bedroomed house in 1906 around the core of a much older building, known as The Bury. Alice Freeman remembered supplying the Grange with cream and butter from the Jersey cow at the Red Lion, and Mrs Willis teaching village girls pillow lace making.

A panoramic view over Heath and Reach, looking towards Baker's Wood and Kings Wood in the far distance, woodland recorded in Domesday Book and now containing Sites of Special Scientific Interest. Much of the village countryside is now scarred with huge sandpits, but in 1841 the census recorded just two sand dealers and ten farmers. Sand was first dug commercially in the village during the late eighteenth century, although field names such as Sand Close occur as far back as 1678. During the nineteenth century the sand industry came to replace the traditional farming economy.

Birds Hill in Heath looking down towards Reach. The village post office is on the right, and is first recorded in a directory of 1853 when William Tompkins is named as postmaster; he was also described as 'baker, flour dealer and farmer'. Note the unusual telephone box, which sadly does not survive. Public telephones were first introduced in 1884 though Heath and Reach had to wait until the early years of this century for its own 'Public Telephone Call Office'.

Rushmere Manor, on the Old Linslade Road, was probably built in 1728 by John Franklin, the Steward to Lord Leigh, who held the Manor of Leighton Buzzard. The grey and red brick house, opposite Rushmere Pond, is marked on Jeffery's map of Bedfordshire in 1755. After the Franklin estates were sold off in the 1820s, the house deteriorated and was divided into cottages for workmen, although today it is once more restored to its original elegance.

Picket Lodge, one of a pair of lodges which once stood next to Rushmere Pond. They framed the entrance gates to Stockgrove Manor, at the crossroads where the Old Linslade Road meets Plantation Road and Brickhill Road. These 'fairy castles' were demolished and replaced with the more utilitarian buildings we see today when Stockgrove House itself was rebuilt in the 1920s.

CHAPTER FOUR

EGGINGTON

This picture appeared in the local paper on 7 June 1966. The caption read: 'Sir Gilbert and Lady Inglefield had just as much fun in pushing the swing as did the occupant – if not more so!' Lady Inglefield, of Eggington House, had just opened the children's playground. Eggington, with the hamlet of Clipstone, was included with Leighton Buzzard in the Domesday Survey of 1086. It was also part of the gift by Henry II to Fontevrault Abbey in France in 1164. The first written reference to Eggington itself was in 1195, and a year later we find a Robert of Clipston recorded.

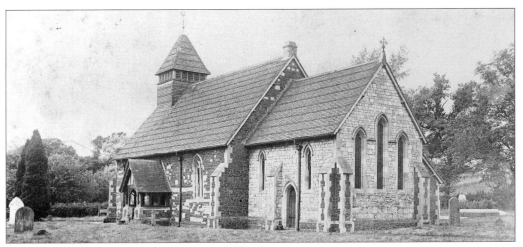

The church of St Michael and All Angels, south side. Until the early part of the nineteenth century (date uncertain, but possibly 1810 or 1837), when it became a separate ecclesiastical parish with its own vicar, Eggington was a dependent chapelry of Leighton Buzzard. Although a church here is mentioned as early as 1273, this building dates from the fourteenth century. It has an Early English chancel and a Decorated nave. According to a glebe terrier made on 25 June 1822, the cupola contained two early bells with the inscriptions 'God save our King, 1622' and 'Anthony Chandler made me, 1677'. The silver communion cup and plate were dated 1635. There was also a folio prayer book and Bible, both printed in 1770. The earliest register is for baptisms for the period 1755 to 1811. Earlier baptisms, marriages and burials are in the Leighton Buzzard registers.

Eggington Church, between 1860 and 1882. This drawing shows the Church House to the left of the picture. In the steward's accounts for 1653 the building is referred to as a curate's house. This building was demolished at the beginning of the twentieth century and the site left vacant until the present vicarage, St Michael's, was built in about 1965. The picture is a copy made by Frederick Gurney of an earlier drawing made in the third quarter of the nineteenth century. Fred was a local antiquarian who, with his brother, lived at Claridges in the village. In 1890 William Claridge, William Smith and John Warner Adams were the main landowners in Eggington.

Interior of St Michael and All Angels, 5 August 1978. In her will (18 September 1537) Elizabeth Brothers of Eggington gave to the Fraternity of Corpus Christi in Leighton Buzzard 7s 4d for her body to be laid out in the brotherhood aisle of All Saints. She also asked for a priest to sing masses for a year for the souls of herself and her friends 'One half year at Leighton and the other half year at Eggington Chapel'.

Chapel and church, with the Horseshoes public house on the right. Mention is made of the Horseshoes in trade directories from 1848, when the landlord was George Horn, although it is sometimes called the Three Horseshoes. It is marked on both the enclosure map of 1840 and the tithe map 1841. Richard Andrews, who died in 1601, had three servants – John Fowler, Williams Hobbes and Agnes Gifford. In his will he left 5s for 'mendynge of the Churchwayes about the Chappell gates and doors'.

The Wesleyan Methodist Chapel. Under an Act of Parliament passed in the reign of George III, rooms used as places of worship by an assembly or congregation of Protestants had to be registered. On 19 April 1861 application was made for this Wesleyan chapel, although it is said to have been built in 1845 for 100 worshippers. As a tablet on the front of the house records, the building was enlarged in 1867 when a balcony was also installed. The chapel closed in 1983 and is now a private house. The earliest mention of Protestant worship in the village is in 1799, when meetings were in the house of William Scroggs. In 1821 the home of William Pantling was being used.

For the Festival of Britain in 1951 all the villages in Bedfordshire were given this pattern of sign; most have survived.

You can just see the other non-conformist chapel in the village in the middle distance in this picture. This was an offshoot of the Hockliffe Congregational Chapel, and was opened on Thursday 12 November 1840. A gallery was added in 1842 and a schoolroom in 1844. Chapel discipline was strict: in 1848 Eliza Ellingham was 'excluded from the Church on account of conduct inconsistent with the Christian character'. In 1851 Ann Pantling was suspended from receiving the Lord's Supper for three months 'on account of having allowed herself to be overcome by strong drink'. From 1844 to 1864 a British School was run from here. The schoolroom measured 23 ft by 16 ft and could hold sixty children. In 1959, after closure, the chapel was sold for about £300 to the British Legion, who converted it for use as a village hall. Later it fell into disrepair and was demolished; Tudor House was built on the site.

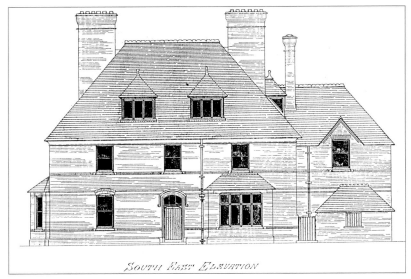

South East Elevation

The White House, south-east elevation, taken from the original plans. Originally this building was known as the New Parsonage House. Later it was called The Vicarage. It was built in 1881–2, the architect being Ewan Christian. From 1951 it became a children's home until cutbacks in the Education Budget in 1982 forced its closure. Now it is a residential home for the elderly. The adjacent stables (now a house called White House Cottage) were completed by April 1885. There was once a row of cottages close to the road in what is now the front garden of The White House and White House Cottage. These were known as The Town Houses and were demolished between about 1840 and 1885. They were part of the estate of the Eggington Town Lands and were later let, with part of the rent used to help the poor and destitute in the parish, or used to provide houses for the homeless of the village.

The White House, Plough Cottage, Church Farm Cottage and Rodells. This view shows one of the former village pubs, The Plough, now called Plough Cottage. It was first licensed in 1836. In a conveyance of 1884 the builder was given as a William Pantling, who at one time may have lived there. He was both a publican and a farmer in the village and built several properties in Eggington. By 1903 the building was in bad repair. When the property was put on the market in 1910 the brewhouse situated over the cellar still contained its brewing copper, mash tub and two beer coolers. It stopped being a pub between 1914 and 1920. There was once a blacksmith working next to the brewhouse.

High Street looking west, 1976. The village school is on the right-hand side. Eggington School was built in 1880 for seventy-five pupils. There was difficulty in obtaining a suitable site and it was several months before Eggington Charity Trustees would agree to sell the land for it. It catered for all ages until about 1945, after which time some of the older children finished their education at schools in Leighton Buzzard. From 1962 the over-eights went to Stanbridge School. By 1979 there were only twelve pupils on the register. After a long hard fight the school eventually closed in the summer of 1983. The building is now used as the village hall.

The Old House, Church Walk, 1980s. This property used to be called Waylands and is one of the few remaining timber-framed houses in the village. A wooden panel on the north gable end at roof level was for access to storage space in the roof. There would have been a hoist so that goods could be winched up from outside. The panel has now been replaced by a small window. There is also a very large oven at one end of the building: was it once a bakehouse?

Manor Cottage, 1995. Manor Cottage was once the demesne or home farm for the small Eggington Manor. The manor consisted of about 160 acres held by undertenants by free tenure, and 80 acres of demesne, the total being about a fifth of the land in the village. There was other manorial land in Eggington but it was attached to other manors, principally that of Grovebury or Leighton Manor. In 1297 Eggington Manor belonged to Henry Child. Of the twenty-seven people in the village paying tax that year Henry was only the seventeenth wealthiest. This manor remained with the Child family at least until 1424, but by 1433 it had passed to the Man family. In the Court Rolls for 1428 sixteen men and one woman are named as 'the tenants and suitors'.

Manor Farm, before the fire on 16 July 1889 which destroyed the west wing. The Man family developed Eggington Manor and eventually were able to build this house, which encroached on what was then the eastern end of the village green. William Man, who died in 1543, left to his son some livestock and all the oak timber which lay 'in the grene before the door'. This may have been the timber he used to build or extend this property. At that date people were most specific in their use of the word 'timber' to denote building material and 'wood' for that used for fuel, making hurdles, tools, wattle panels, furniture and so on. The man on the pony cart is Ezra Batchelar, died 1912. He was the son of Gaius and Elizabeth Batchelar; the family farmed extensively in the village and surrounding area. It was with the Batchelar family that the court rolls for the manor ended up.

The east end of the village before the ravages of Dutch Elm disease. Manor Farm, on the left, was only partially rebuilt after a fire in 1889. Eggington House can be seen to the right, beyond the photographer's car.

Eggington House and its Lodge. The message on this card reads: 'Dear Nell, I am sending you a photo of our nursery, this is where I live.' To the left of this picture, behind Manor Farm, an archaeological dig took place in 1972; finds were made from the Roman, Saxon and Medieval periods. This was close to where in 1932, whilst digging sand, a skeleton and pottery from the second century had been unearthed.

The balloon has landed, at the rear of Eggington House – said to have been built in 1694 for John Renouille. He was a Merchant Taylor and Huguenot from Montauban in France, trading from Holborn. In 1728 the house was occupied by Richard Gurney. On John's death – some time before 1738 – the property went to his son John James Reynal (the Anglicized form of the surname), who was given a grant of arms in 1737. The family lived in Hockliffe Manor House and let Eggington House. On the death of John James in 1767, his son John was aged nineteen. In 1777 this John became Sheriff of Bedfordshire; he died before his wife Sarah, who then married Francis Moore. By 1840 the estate belonged to the Adams family.

Eggington House. The house has a fine staircase with oak twist balusters. At the turn of the century it was owned by the Hodgson family, friends of Sylvia Pankhurst, the suffragette, who used to stay here. During the First World War it was requisitioned for army accommodation. The house was the home of Sir Gilbert Inglefield and his family from 1950 until 1976. In 1967–8 Sir Gilbert was Lord Mayor of London, and one of the local Middle Schools is named in his honour. Sir Gordon Slynn and his wife Odile were the next owners. Coincidentally Lady Slynn also came here from Montauban, via Holborn.

Mr Mead, the baker from Stanbridge with Bess, at the gates of Eggington House. The village horses were usually from London. They could be bought cheaply as their feet became tender from walking on the cobbles and they had to be retired. After careful treatment on the local soft ground and feeding up they would improve, and had years of useful life left in them. The animals came by train and were unloaded at Dunstable as Stanbridgeford only catered for cattle.

Post office and village shop, 1976. By 1861 the village had a postmaster, William Southam, whose fourteen-year-old son Frederick worked as a labourer at one of the local brickworks, possibly Prior's Yard; this was run by Charles Prior, Master Brickmaker from Ongar in Essex. David and Ann Stevens were owners from about 1850 to 1894. David, who ran it as a grocery shop, was also the village carrier. In 1910 the shop was sold by the executors of John Adams and a Mr Leach remained tenant until his death, when Sarah Leach took over the running of the business. The single-storey extension was added by Arthur Bowerman. After the business closed in 1979 the extension was demolished, and the property renamed Well Cottage.

High Street, opposite the church, looking east. In this view one can see Plough Cottage, Church Farm Cottage and Rodells, with the single-storey extension which was demolished when Church Walk was made. Henry Edwards, who died in 1894 aged seventy-four, ran a carpentry business from this single-storey building. Church Farm Cottage was the building from which at one time all the holdings of the Town Lands Charity were farmed. The property is itemized in a rental of 1589 that fixes the building to this position. At the end of the nineteenth century the farmer was William Saunders, the Knacker Man, who had a slaughterhouse here.

Garden of The Meadows, at the junction of Charity Lane, Orchard Estate. Behind 11–13 Orchard Estate is Pit Field, which in 1840 was owned by William Smith. From 1846 to 1888 Charles Prior rented 4 acres of this field for a brickworks, where the yellow-coloured bricks called Eggington Greys were made. These bricks can be seen on many of the local buildings. There was also a small railway to move goods around the site. One very interesting will, for Agnes Doggett, dated 4 June 1614, survives. She makes her husband overseer of her will giving him all her bees for his pains. One usually only finds spinsters and widows making wills at this date; a married woman had to have her husband's permission as he owned her and all her possessions. We don't yet know where exactly in the village they lived; could it be somewhere near here?

Guinevere Elizabeth Batchelar, with pram, plays in the garden of West Hill, Leighton Road, *c.* 1934. Leighton Road at one time was called West Lane. In 1850 John Batchelar, Guinevere's great-great-grandfather, was Overseer of the Poor for Eggington. His son Gaius followed in his father's footsteps and for sixty-three years was the Eggington representative on the Board (or Ward) of Guardians for the Union Workhouse in Leighton Buzzard.

Haydon House, a Batchelar farmhouse built in the 1950s. As one senior citizen remembers: 'Mr Batchelar delivered all of his milk to Ted Newens in Hartwell Grove, Leighton Buzzard by pony and trap and later in an old RAF van.' Eggington has always been a farming community. In his will of 15 February 1787 Joseph Eames, farmer, asked his brother Joshua Janes living in Eggington, and John Ellingham, farmer of Clipstone, to be trustees for his children whom he wanted to continue in his farming business. He instructs them what to do if 'they find my Children waste and Destroy the stock in Business'. In 1861 there were seven men in the village who described themselves as shepherds. Eighty people were engaged in plaiting straw, and there were three plait dealers in the village.

CHAPTER FIVE

STANBRIDGE

School and chapel. The earliest record of non-conformity in the village of Stanbridge is in September 1795, when permission was sought in the Archdeaconry Court to use a room in the house of Nicholas Lucas for worship. On 7 July 1817 John Tearle applied for permission for 'a congregation of Protestants' to be allowed to meet in his home.

The parish church is dedicated to St John the Baptist and was built in about 1270. In the fifteenth century clerestory windows were added to the nave. The present organ was installed in 1928. The original five bells, which had dates of 1637, 1709, 1725, 1755 and 1807, were rehung in 1951. A sixth treble bell was added to the peal in 1988. Inside on the north wall of the chancel is a memorial to Henry Honner, who died in 1627, and Jane his wife, who died two years later. Henry left 'Bell Rope Field' to pay for the upkeep of the ropes in the belfry. A plan for the modernization of the church was drawn up, in 1879, by Ewan Christian, but the work was not carried out until 1892–3.

This is a view of the church interior before restoration work, which was completed in 1892–3 when the Revd Thomas Green was vicar. Several of the bills and receipts for this work have survived and are in the County Record Office at Bedford. In his will of 1548 Thomas Bawdrey requested that when the mourners gathered in the church a month after his death (called his month's mind) to say prayers for his soul, they were to be given bread, cheese and ale at his expense. If his grave was inside the church, as seems likely, it would have been left open until this ceremony had taken place.

Stanbridge was a chapelry of Leighton Buzzard until, in 1844, with Gregory Edward Whyley as its first incumbent, it became a vicariate. The creation of the United Benefice of Stanbridge with Tilsworth took place in 1871. In 1980 Totternhoe joined them, and on 1 December 1982 the parishes of Stanbridge, Tilsworth, Totternhoe, Eaton Bray with Dagnall, Whipsnade, Studham and Kensworth were formed into the North Chilterns Group, served by three incumbents.

The village was one of thirty-one 'Thankful Villages' in the country, which were able to welcome home all fifty of their men who had fought in the First World War. To commemorate this happy event the village installed a clock on the west face of the church tower. The parish was not so fortunate in the Second World War, as five villagers are named as casualties on the memorial in the church. They are M.C. Hedges, J. Kempster, V. Sells, K. Stanbridge and E. Ward. For Christmas 1994 the clock was illuminated by installing floodlighting for the west face of the tower. The light was switched on for the first time by Anthony Briggs, Chairman of the Parish Council.

Ellingham memorial. Not surprisingly, in view of the twelve surviving children Daniel and Elizabeth had, wills for several members of the Ellingham family have survived. In that of another Daniel, who died in 1754, the house he lived in was to be shared between his son Gabriel and daughter Sarah. She was to have the parlour, the best room and the little cellar until she married. Another relation, Francis White, who was married to a Mary Ellingham (he died in about 1765) had a flock of ninety sheep on his freehold farm in Stanbridge. James Hill, a schoolmaster teaching in Leighton Buzzard, married Judith Ellingham of Stanbridge in 1712. In 1725 James died and was buried in All Saints, L.B. The Daniel on the memorial had been a churchwarden, and in 1683 gave a silver communion cup to the parish.

The Old Vicarage, Mill Road. This house was built in 1874 to the plans of the architect Ewan Christian. At Stanbridge children would pick primroses from the large vicarage garden to make posies for Mothering Sunday. The garden is not so extensive now, as in 1966 the new vicarage was built next door. The Sunday School treat at Stanbridge in the 1940s was either afternoon tea and games on the vicarage lawn or an outing by coach to Clacton or Southend, starting at six in the morning and returning in the late evening.

The Wesleyan Methodist Chapel, Mill Road. This chapel was registered by John Cooper on 30 August 1870. Part was demolished, probably in about January 1972, when its registration was cancelled; the rest was incorporated into Chapel House. The two gate piers seen in this picture are the only external evidence now.

This is the Primitive Methodist Chapel, Tilsworth Road, which was registered on 9 January 1861 by Matthew Plummer of Luton, a bonnet maker who was one of the trustees of the chapel. It was here that the first school was held in the village in June 1876. The fee was 2*d* a week at first but soon rose to 4*d*. Holidays were four weeks a year, taken to coincide with harvest when the children would be needed on the farms. The new school was built adjacent to the chapel in 1881. In 1885 the school log book recorded that 'Many children are absent this afternoon. Most are gathering cowslips.' It was customary for herbs and flowers to be collected by children and sold to supplement the family income.

This was how the village school looked when Miss Gladys Mary Watling worked there, from 1930 to 1935. She was a local girl from Leighton Buzzard and was said at the time to have been the youngest headmistress in Bedfordshire. Irene Flowerday who later became Mrs Baker, of Dunstable, was one of the pupil teachers here in the 1930s.

A view of Stanbridge school which will be familiar to present-day children. The brick wall on the right has now been demolished and modern classrooms added. The school now takes infants from Eggington, Billington and Tilsworth as well as Stanbridge. The other villages originally had schools of their own, catering for children of all ages.

School group, *c.* 1910. A school in Stanbridge was opened in June 1876 in the Primitive Methodist Chapel. It catered for all ages of children and its maximum capacity was eighty. A new school was built next door in 1881. A new wing was built in 1961 and a playing field added by levelling the earthworks in Great Bury Close. These lumps and bumps together with those in Little Bury Close were probably the remains of the garden, fishponds and dovehouse of the manor, documented in 1291. The mill at this early period was on the hill-top here, and only later was it moved to the Mill Road site.

School group, *c.* 1920. Mr Samuel C. DeLamont, seen here with a group of the older children, died on 27 June 1931 aged seventy-three. He had been schoolmaster at Stanbridge for thirty-eight years, coming to the school in 1883 and retiring in 1921. Samuel was born in St Helier, Jersey. His wife Mary, a Wolverhampton girl, also taught for a time at the school. They had at least two children, Marion and Samuel. In 1861 the village schoolmaster was John Ellingham, aged twenty-nine, who had come here from Hayes, Middlesex. He lived in Peddars Lane with his thirty-five-year-old wife Ann, a local girl from Tilsworth, and their three young children. At this time John would probably have taught in the local church, chapel or a room in his own house.

Chapel and post office, 16–18 Tilsworth Road, *c.* 1915. The Primitive Methodist Chapel is on the left. The chimney of Laurel Cottage, 40 Tilsworth Road, can just be seen over the top of the trees on the opposite side of the road. The cottage would have been next to one of the village ponds. Before the age of the car it was vital to have water available at the roadside for the horses. In most villages there was at least one pond where animals could drink. Some of those in Stanbridge had carp in them. A Stanbridge baker recalls the summer of 1921 when, one by one, they all dried up, the fish died and water had to be brought into the village. The baker bought a holding tank from a local farmer and until Christmas made daily trips to Leighton with his horse and cart, returning with three churns of water. In 1955 the parish council sold one of the ponds to Bedfordshire County Council Highways Department for the princely sum of 5s so they could widen the road.

Chapel and post office, *c.* 1920. Today this view has fewer trees and more houses. By the 1950s, however, the village atmosphere was under threat; in autumn 1956 the Minister of Housing and Local Government announced his decision on the development of the area. The plan for a new town of 50,000 people at Stanbridge was rejected – Milton Keynes got that honour! The building on the right is now the village shop and post office. In 1885 there was no post office in the village, but there was a wall box which was emptied at 6 p.m. each weekday. By 1894 Levi Stevens had become the village sub-postmaster.

This house, 33 Tilsworth Road, is said to have been built in about 1912 by William Clarke, a local carpenter, builder and undertaker. The firm were the funeral directors when Mrs Sarah Ward Franklin died in January 1912 aged eighty-four. Her family had been connected with the village for many years.

Corner of Mill Road and Tilsworth Road; Church Farm is on the right. Church Farm, the house, is thought to have been built in 1851. In 1882 a Mr Gurney sold it to Mr Littleboy. Thirty years later it was on the market again and was purchased by Mr Costin. The farm itself with all its fields can be traced back to 1697. In 1913 the Griffin family, who were tenant farmers, moved from here to Old Farm in Station Road. In 1922 Jack and Ron Griffin, who later started an electrical firm in Leighton Buzzard, were experimenting with radio and were among the first people to receive a live broadcast from America.

Wedding Belles, Dunstable Methodist Church, 18 July 1929. The groom, Dennis Charles Mead, until 1964 the baker in Stanbridge, was born in Wingrave, Buckinghamshire, on 11 May 1904. He was one of ten children and came to live in the village in 1910. In 1929 he married Lily Cheshire, who at the time worked in a tobacconist's shop in Middle Row. They had met through the chapel, and the happy marriage was to last sixty years. Back row, left to right: Edward Mead, Lizzie Mead, Dennis Bignall, Lucy Cheshire, Alfred Cheshire, Dorothy Cheshire. Front row: Renee Cheshire, Connie Mead, Dennis Mead, Lily Cheshire, Grace Cheshire, Phyllis Cheshire.

Baker's van outside Bakers Cottage, 21 Tilsworth Road. Dennis Mead left school at fourteen. At first he worked for Mr Heady in Mill Road, Stanbridge, but eventually went into business for himself. He baked on these premises in coal-fired ovens which were later converted to oil. The working day started at four in the morning – earlier at holiday times. Bread deliveries, to all the villages, at first were by pony and trap but in 1934 Mr Mead bought a Morris van: the price was £120 on the road. After Mr Mead's retirement in 1964 the business was continued for another ten years by Mr Gorham until he left for Wales.

STANBRIDGE, BEDS

CATALOGUE OF

52 SHEEP and LAMBS,

2 CART HORSES,

PONY, NAG MARE,

BLACK COW (in full profit),

6 YEARLING HEIFERS,

A QUANTITY OF

AGRICULTURAL IMPLEMENTS

HARNESS, &c.

AND

3 ORCHARDS OF FRUIT,

TO BE SOLD BY AUCTION, BY MESSRS.

Stafford, Rogers & A. W. Merry
Ltd.,

On Thursday, Aug. 7, 1919,

At 3 o'clock precisely, by direction of Mr. G W. Olney.

The Sale will take place at The White House Farm premises near Tilsworth.

Catalogues may be obtained of the Auctioneers, Leighton Buzzard, Bedford and Newport Pagnell.

Rush & Warwick, Printers, Leighton Buzzard

Sale catalogue, 7 August 1919. There were many fruit orchards in the village and plum trees can still be found growing in the hedgerows. In late summer the fruit was sold at auction whilst still on the trees. Buyers, often from London, would use casual labour to pick the fruit which was put into locally made baskets, often those of Messrs Robinson, Leighton Buzzard, and sent to market on the train from Stanbridgeford station. Orchard Close reminds us that after the last war, when fruit growing became uneconomical, the orchards were often sold for house-building.

Green Farm. William Edwins senior, of Green Farm, Stanbridge, died on Saturday 20 January 1912 aged eighty-two. He was 'stalwart in Liberalism and Primitive Methodism'. The name Green Farm has also been attached to other farms in the village. In June 1886 the Bunker family came to live at Ivy Farm, Station Road. At that time Ivy Farm, together with Home Close, Peddars Lane and Green Farm, were farmed as one unit.

The Festival of Britain village sign. It is hoped that all these signs will be refurbished for the millennium.

The Wheatsheaf, now Wheatsheaf House, Leighton Road (on the left), dates from about 1840. It ceased being a pub in 1958. Mr George Giltrow was the last landlord and he lived here for about fifty-two years. Before 1914 a Statty or Hiring Fair was held here each year in the autumn. In 1861 Jesse Giltrow, born in 1847, was living with John Franklin and his family. The Franklins at that time were farming about 300 acres, one of the largest farms in the village. Jesse was employed as a 'bucket boy'.

The Five Bells at the junction of Leighton Road, Station Road, The Green and Tilsworth Road. In 1841 John and Jane Tomkins, with their new baby Sarah, were living at the Five Bells. John was a tailor as well as a publican. In about 1842 Joseph Eames and his first wife Elizabeth and their family moved here. Mr Eames died on 28 April 1895 aged eighty-three. At the time Joseph was said to be the oldest licensed victualler in Bedfordshire. He was also a cattle dealer and always wore a tall hat and braided smock when he went into town. On the Tuesday preceding his death he had attended Leighton Market as usual, and it was on his return home that he was taken ill. His widow Alice Sarah took over the pub until about 1905. The next landlord was Philip Olney, who was also a butcher. The Olney family also had the Red Lion in the village. Later landlords include Stanley Arthur Williams and Richard John Dauncy. The meetings of the first school board for Stanbridge, Tilsworth and Eggington were held here in 1874.

STANDBRIDGE, BEDS.

Messrs. HART & SON

Are instructed by Mr. John Gurney

TO SELL BY AUCTION,

At the Five Bells Inn, Standbridge, On THURSDAY, THE 14TH OF NOVEMBER, 1889, At Four o'Clock in the Afternoon, a valuable small

FREEHOLD PROPERTY,

SITUATE as above, abutting on the High Road from Standbridge to the London and North-Western Railway Station and Eaton Bray, consisting of a brick-built and slated HOUSE, with iron pallisade in front, having two rooms and wash-house, with copper, on the ground floor, and three bed-rooms and an attic over; adjoining is a brick-built and slated wood-house, closet, and a pump and well of water. There is also a part brick and part timber-built and tiled building, formerly used as a blacksmith's shop. At rear is an ORCHARD, with a brick-built and slated pigstye, and a timber-built and tiled fowl-house and pigstye, the whole having an area of about forty perches.

It is now in the occupation of the County Police, and is let at the low rental of £9 10s. per annum. Outgoings, Land-tax, 6s. Vicar's Tithe, 2s.

It is bounded on the north-west by property belonging to Richard Littleboy, Esq., and on the south and south-east by property belonging to Mr. Richard Knight.

Conditions will be read at the time of Sale.

Messrs. F. and D. T. Willis,

Hart and Son, Auction Offices, Leighton Buzzard.

Solicitors, Leighton Buzzard.

Sale particulars, 3 Tilsworth Road, 14 November 1889. The present police house is at the other end of the village at 70 Tilsworth Road, on the south side of the road just before the Red Lion. In 1871 the parish constables were S. Timms and W. Horne, but where they lived is not known.

1 and 3 Tilsworth Road. The blacksmith's forge referred to in the sale was for many years run by the Twigg family on the premises to the right of this photograph, at 5 Tilsworth Road.

Road mender, with Totternhoe Knolls in the background. One couldn't stand here now as it is part of the Leighton Buzzard bypass. Thomas Honour (the Honour memorial is on the north wall of the chancel of the parish church) who died in 1564 or 1565, absolved his dues to God and the parish by requesting in his will that his executors 'lay 10 loads of white stones and 10 loads of flints in the highway where most needed'. For many years it was the responsibility of each parish to mend its own roads.

Stanbridgeford station, with the crossing keeper's house on the right. The line from Leighton Buzzard to Luton had its first stop here. Opened in 1848, the line was carrying an average of 242 passengers on the first train of the day before 1914. By the 1960s, however, it was considered to be uneconomical. At the end of June 1962 hundreds of local people gathered at Leighton Buzzard station to bid farewell to the Dunstable Dasher, as the passenger train on this line was called after Dr Beeching's axe fell on it. Driver Harry Crossley, with fireman T. Daniels and guard Percy Dimmock, brought the train, decorated with streamers and carrying a wreath presented by Bob Cook, Chairman of the Linslade Urban District Council, into Leighton Buzzard station. They were three-quarters of an hour early but found eighty passengers waiting to board. When the train left the number had risen to 300. At Stanbridgeford station sixteen Women's Institute members from Eaton Bray were patiently waiting to join the train. The station stayed open for freight for a further two years but finally closed on 1 June 1964.

CHAPTER SIX

BILLINGTON

Billington parish church, St Michael and All Angels, built in the late thirteenth century on the very top of Billington hill, the Anglo-Saxon 'dun' from which its name is derived. This water colour of the church was painted by George Shepherd between 1810 and 1820. It shows the old church before the addition of the bell turret.

St Michael's is seen here after its Victorian restoration in 1869; the bell turret came from St Barnabas's Church at Linslade, where it had been replaced with a tower. The taxation of 1297, when the chapel was newly built, gives as Billington's first named residents: John and William Lancroft, Walter and Henry North, John Harding, Ernulph Bowyere, William Liverich, Walter ate Hulle, Cristina de Pratis, William Wodeward, Simon Bullocherde, Robert Ordwy and Henry Lepere. The surnames indicate various occupations from bow-making to wood warden and cow herding. Walter ate Hulle probably lived 'on the hill', the main settlement around today's church.

The interior of the church, 1905. The modern east window is set in fifteenth-century stonework. In 1557 Alis Morley left money in her will ' . . . to Billington Chappell to helpe to by a rooffe 5s'.

Billington Sunday School and churchgoers outside St Michael's, 1939. Among those pictured are Nurse Burchell, Brenda Price, Roland Brandom, Joan, Evelyn and Margery Andrews, Connie Pittam, Vernon Price, Ruby Smith, Bernard Smith, Dick Spratley, Doug Mason, Nelson Mason, Mrs Holmes, Miss Morgan, Miss Tatt, Mrs Lee, Miss Olney, Mr Spratley, Mr Tatt, Mrs Spratley and Bill Evans.

The Huxley family bought Billington Manor from the Jackmans in 1636, their main seat being at nearby Eaton Bray. This faint thumbnail sketch from William Gordon's map of the county in 1736 shows their coat of arms and perhaps the manor house.

In 1881 Arthur Macnamara rebuilt the Manor as a fitting residence for his wife Lady Sophia, daughter of an Earl and lady of the bedchamber to the Princess Louise, one of Queen Victoria's younger daughters.

The lovely gardens and lakes at Billington Manor welcomed Princess Louise in July 1886, when she stayed with the Macnamaras during her visit to mark the re-opening of the restored All Saints' Church in Leighton Buzzard.

Another Royal visitor was Edward, Prince of Wales, later Duke of Windsor. He hunted with the Rothschilds in the district and in 1924 broke his collar bone jumping fences at the Manor. The stables, seen here, were later used for village parties.

Macnamara died a bankrupt in 1906, and the Manor was sold in 1910. He is buried alone in Billington churchyard; Lady Sophia died in 1912 and her remains were buried in Ireland according to her wishes. They had no children. In July 1919 Sir Richard and Lady Cooper entertained villagers to Peace Festivities in the manor grounds, with 250 people sitting down to dinner.

The afternoon was devoted to sports, causing much amusement. This was followed by tea and an evening of music.

The coronation of George V in June 1911 was celebrated in style in Billington, when about 200 villagers sat down to dinner in the 'capacious coach-house' of the Manor. Captain J. Babington Gilliatt had bought the Manor the previous October, and he and his wife were thanked for their hospitality. After singing the national anthem the children played games and sports under the watchful eye of the village schoolmistress Miss Finch. Tea was followed by a tug-of-war between Great and Little Billington, resulting in victory for the latter. A concert and other revelry went on until nearly midnight. Among the children pictured in this photograph are Dossie Evans, Elsie Smith, Dolly, Lucy and Ada Andrews, Kate Holmes, Violet Reed, Daisy and Jessie Griffin, Annie and Edie Ashby, May Foster and Ada, Gwen Roff, Kate Betts and sister, Triphena Mann, Georgina Mann, Selina Mann, Freda Hemley, and two Willard sisters.

A village Women's Institute party in the hall over the Stables, c. 1950. The photograph includes Mrs Grugeon, J. Fountaine, Mrs Hervey, Mrs Brunning, Miss Tinsley, Miss Andrews, Lil Tatt, Miss Millins, R. O'Dell, Mrs Smith, Miss Morgan, Joyce Smith, Mrs Knapit, R. Hervey, B. Fountaine, E. Smith, Mrs Kingett, Tom Spratley, Mr and Mrs S. Tearle, Janet Roff and Mrs Roff.

Looking up Billington Hill from the Stanbridge Road junction at the south end of the village. The school can be seen at the top of the road in this photograph, which dates from about 1920. When the officers of the Bishop of Lincoln visited the village in 1717 they reported that there was 'no school endowed but children are taught to read and learn the church catechism by a poor woman'.

The Education Returns of 1833 also reported that no school existed in the village. By 1847 there was a Sunday School for twelve boys and ten girls but in a 'very unsettled state' owing to the ruinous condition of the chapel. But in 1863 the National School was built and was teaching eighty children their lessons by 1870. This photograph from the 1950s was taken inside the classroom and shows the teacher Mrs Kingett, with Len Ward, Olive Smith, Brian Smith, Valerie Jaggard, Sylvia Tearle, Terry Millins and Tony Cox among her pupils.

A class poses on the school steps, 1927. From the back, left to right: Miss Levesly, Florrie Ritchie, Icky Saunders, Eric Cox, Dick Spratley, Ray Page, Jack Sear, Arthur Murgett, Leslie Roff, Reg Roff, Mildred Beasley, ? Saunders, Daphne Stone, Jack Stone, Norman Head, ? Saunders, Edie Cox, Mildred Ritchie. As with many village schools attendance varied with the seasons, since the children were a useful source of labour in a farming community. The school logbook records a plait school — producing straw plait for hats — in the village in 1875, and also notes that in 1885 Alfred Gatwood, a Billington labourer, was summoned for assaulting the School Attendance Officer in the execution of his duty.

The stars of the nativity play performed by Billington schoolchildren at Leighton vicarage, 1937. Back row, left to right: John Head, Lionel Fountaine, Dennis O'Dell, Billy Champion. Middle row: Ursula ?, Ken Champion, Evelyn Andrews, Vernon Price, Olive Murgett, Spencer Fountaine, Bernard Smith, Margery Andrews. Front row: Billy Edwins, Jill Stone, Doreen Maynard, Brenda Price, Fred Fountaine, Eileen Maynard.

Until the late 1860s Billington was a chapelry under All Saints' Parish Church in Leighton Buzzard. A curate or minister was paid out of the Town Lands Charity, which also paid for repairs to the minister's house, and to the Chapel House, which gave a home to poor families. After Billington became a parish in its own right, the rectory pictured here was built next to the church.

Billington schoolchildren in 1921. Among those pictured are Phyllis Vallender, Cecil Dudley. Violet Reid, Rose Sanders, Tom Spratley, Ivy Menenger, Florrie Sanders, Albert Beasley, Alec Scott, Bill Smith, Maud Reid, Clem Stone, Kath Page, Gladys Stone, Bill Cox, Jim Ashby, Charley Spratley, Mark Spratley, Nellie Fountain, Doris Reid and Cis Roff. The school expanded during the Second World War when sixty evacuees came to stay at the Manor and attended the village school. It closed a few years later.

Maps of the village from the last century show that the fields round the Recreation Ground were all orchards. This photograph shows one of the oldest village houses, set back from Gaddesdon Row, and called The Orchards. Billington grew a particular variety of plum, which became known as the Billington Plum, used as a dye in the straw hat industry, as well as for jam making.

In the early spring of 1592, four years after the defeat of the Spanish Armada, Anne Tomkyns lay dying in Billington. On 21 February she made her will, carefully listing her few possessions: 'to Agnis his wyfe my syster a gown cloth & a gown ready made & a Red petycote'. The two witnesses to her will were 'Wylliam Hogg dwelling on the hill and Wylliam Hogg dwelling beneth the hill'. This old photograph from the 1920s shows Hill Top Farm on the summit of Billington Hill, perhaps the house that the first William Hogg lived in.

Hervey's Cottage, which sits on the Leighton Road facing the church, 1970s. Today this lovely old house is a highly prized residence, but 100 years ago its occupants were probably a farm labourer and his family.

Stanley Andrews with his dog, standing in front of Hervey's cottage in the 1920s.

One of the cottages on Little Hill, which have now been demolished.

In July 1838 George Garrett of Little Gaddesden, Hertfordshire, paid James and Valentine Leach £1,375 for 'a messuage with outbuildings and about 68 acres in the open fields in Billington, and eight single cow commons on Summerlays'. This was Green Farm, pictured above in the 1920s, which had been known as Lower Farm, Great Billington. When the open fields were enclosed between 1844 and 1848 the land was allotted close to the farmhouse; nearby was The Green, with Gaddesden Row running round it.

Village children pose with their pony in Walkers Farm yard.

In the 1950s fire destroyed two thatched cottages despite Leighton Buzzard Fire Brigade rushing to the scene, and draining the seventeenth-century moat at Manor Farm. St Margarets Cottage and Orchard Cottage stood on the corner of Stanbridge Road and Northall Road; the occupants at the time were Mrs Pearce and her son Edward, and Mrs Olney and her daughter Edith. Mrs Pearce noticed the fire while hanging out washing.

The post office on the hill down into Leighton, with two adjoining cottages. In 1853 Craven & Co.'s Directory reported 'Letters received irregularly', and the 1869 one declared 'There is a pillar post cleared at 6.30 a.m.'. In 1885 letters were still received via Leighton Buzzard, but by 1894 Billington had its own post office, with Mrs Elizabeth Thompson the sub-postmistress.

By 1914 Alfred Shaw was Billington's sub-postmaster and he is seen on the right of this photograph standing outside his post office. In the cottage doorway on the left are Elsie Smith and her mother, with Bill Smith and his grandmother standing at the gate. At the gate in the centre is Sarah Miles.

Mr Shaw was still the postmaster in 1924, and the post office did not close until the 1970s. He also ran the village shop, and is seen here in later life with his three great nieces Joan, Evelyn and Margery Andrews.

Walkers Farm on the Leighton Road at Billington, pictured in the early part of this century. It is said that Charley Spratley bought the farm for £1,000 in gold sovereigns from William Labrum in 1917. The field running alongside the road between the farmhouse and the church, known as Packman's Close, is recorded as far back as 1664; its name probably refers to the packhorses which used the road.

In 1841 the seventy-five-year-old Thomas Stevens lived at Walkers Farm with his wife and family, but it was later bought by Arthur Macnamara of Billington Manor, and his stone monogram 'AM' adorns the outside wall to this day.

In April 1926 Billington saw the funeral of Leading Aircraftsman Basil Young, who was buried with full military honours. He had been killed on 10 April in an aircraft disaster at Henlow Aerodrome, which claimed five lives. The photograph shows the funeral cortège going up Billington Hill after assembling outside the post office. The coffin, covered by a Union Jack, followed the band of the Royal Air Force, formed just eight years before, and among the mourners were forty men of the RAF including Wing Commanders and Squadron Leaders. LAC Young, who was only twenty-three, was buried to the sound of the Last Post and volleys fired over his grave. A wreath of lilies was inscribed: 'For England, Home and Duty, the white flower of a blameless life.'

The view from the top of Billington Hill looking south. In the centre left of the picture can be seen the old Primitive Methodist chapel, with the village school facing the road.

The Primitive Methodists first met at Billington in 1848, holding their meetings in a house until the building of their chapel. The 1851 religious census recorded a congregation of thirty-two in the morning and seventy in the evening – even though the chapel only had seats for forty-five with room for a further twenty-five standing. The tiny hill-top chapel survived as a place of worship for a hundred years. It was used as a garage in the 1950s and today a new house stands on the site. The Wesleyan Methodists built their chapel at the bottom of the hill in Gaddesden Row, where it still stands today, now used as a private house.

In the 1891 census Billington had a grocer's shop, a general shop, and a baker, Joseph Evans from Slapton. Joseph, who was twenty-four, lived with his wife Emmie, aged twenty-eight, and his thirteen-year-old apprentice Able Peek. In the 1924 Directory Joseph is listed in Little Billington, and the old bakery cottage is now called Homeside. The Evans family emigrated to New Zealand, where they are reported to have grown Billington plums! This photograph shows Dossie and Mabel Evans.

Another Slapton family that moved into Little Billington was the Roffs, who were farmers. In 1871 Thomas Roff was farming in a small way with just 10 acres, and ten years later described himself as just a 'tractor engine driver'. By the date of the next census he had died, leaving his widow Mary Ann farming with the help of her two unmarried daughters Alice and Ellen, and eighteen-year-old son William. In the farmhouse next door lived her married son George with his young family. Spring Farm at Little Billington, where the Roffs possibly lived, was sold at auction in 1937, and today another family of Roffs farms at Spring Meadow Farm in Little Billington. The photograph shows 'Granny Roff', probably the widowed Mary Ann.

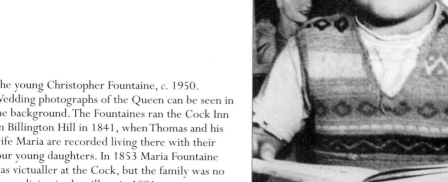

The young Christopher Fountaine, c. 1950. Wedding photographs of the Queen can be seen in the background. The Fountaines ran the Cock Inn on Billington Hill in 1841, when Thomas and his wife Maria are recorded living there with their four young daughters. In 1853 Maria Fountaine was victualler at the Cock, but the family was no longer living in the village in 1891.

Birchells Cottages at Little Billington, built between 1840 and 1850. In 1888 the four brick and slated cottages, together with other property, were sold for £200, and were then occupied by George Holmes, David Henley, Alfred King and George Burchell. They were again sold in 1894 for £125, by which time George's son William Burchell, with his wife Lydia and their six young children, also had one of the cottages.

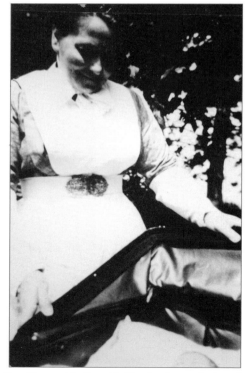

These two photographs from 1927 show Nurse Burchell, the village midwife, with Mrs Sanders and a brand new villager in his pram. She may have been one of William Burchell's two daughters, Lizzie or Jane.

Billington Cricket Club reformed after the First World War and drew up a team to play other villages. This photograph was taken in 1920. Back row, left to right: Harry King, Jack Roff, Ernie Holmes, Stan Millins, Mark Spratley, Cecil Dudley. Middle row: Jack Scott, Alfred Shaw. Front row: Teddy Geeves, William Smith, Jimmy Smith. The team used to play in Green, now Ward, Field, Green Farm.

The village cricket team after the Second World War, in Clem Adams Field, 1947–8. Back row, left to right: Lofty Reynolds, Tony Sinfield, Les Roff, Ken Garner, Stan Millins, Lawrence Fountaine. Front row: Clem Adams, Tom Spratley, David Fountaine, W. Fountaine, Brian Edwards, Peter Flatt.

This photograph from 1939 shows Billington's own 'Dad's Army', members of the Local Defence Volunteer Home Guard, digging a trench on the top of Billington Hill. During the war the village provided both a safe haven for evacuees and a prisoner-of-war camp.

The village pancake race in Hillview Lane, c. 1960. The two contestants and onlookers are Captain Smith, Will O'Dell, Henry Franks, Brian Smith, Tony Smith and Christine Garner. Hillview Lane follows the old line of the hollow way which carried the road through the village to Leighton. The sharp bend at the bottom of the steep hill was straightened following increased motor traffic during the past forty years.

One of Billington's two pubs, this thatched house was once the Cock Inn. In July 1788 William Coleman of Billington left the Cock to his nephew Thomas, a yeoman who also lived in the village. The landlady was Allis Humble. By 1841 the Fountaine family were running the pub, followed by the Pratts, and when it closed in the 1920s its landlord was William Windmill.

The Greyhound Inn in Little Billington at the junction of the roads to Slapton and Leighton Buzzard. It is named from the beginning of the nineteenth century and was run by Thomas Squires from the 1850s to the 1870s, and then by his widow Catherine. In 1914 a valuation was taken of the fixtures, furniture, trade utensils and stock at the inn, and these included a dartboard and darts, a ringboard and rings, three enamelled spittoons, spouted quart and pint jugs and a box of dominoes. The total value, including fruit in the orchard and a ladder, was £16 1s 9d.

ACKNOWLEDGEMENTS

This book could not have been produced without the help of many local people and friends who have given generously of their time and expertise. The authors would like to thank all those who have loaned photographs for the book: Sandra Bagot, the Revd W.E. Barrow, Bedfordshire County Record Office, Billington Parish Council, Buckinghamshire County Record Office, Guinevere Calder, Stephen Coleman, Sue Collins, Alice Freeman, Friends of St Mary's, Margaret and Eric Guess, Druuske Hawkridge, Colin Holmes, Roy Humphries, Tom Lawson, Leighton Buzzard Library, *Leighton Buzzard Observer*, Leighton Linslade Town Council, the Mead family, Margaret Randall, Val and Alan Scott, and William Yirrell.

BRITAIN IN OLD PHOTOGRAPHS

SUTTON'S PHOTOGRAPHIC HISTORY OF TRANSPORT

To order any of these titles please telephone our distributor, Littlehampton Book Services on 01903 828800
For a catalogue of these and our other titles please ring Regina Schinner on 01453 731114